STUCK
IN A SMALL
WORLD

STEVE WYATT

STUCK
IN A SMALL
WORLD

Staying on Board with Your Not-So-Unique

Yet Thoroughly Dysfunctional Family

Standard®
PUBLISHING
Bringing The Word to Life

Cincinnati, Ohio

Published by Standard Publishing, Cincinnati, Ohio
www.standardpub.com

Project editor: Lynn Lusby Pratt
Cover and interior design: studiogearbox.com

ISBN 978-0-7847-2111-7

Library of Congress Cataloging-in-Publication Data

Wyatt, Stephen T. (Stephen Thomas), 1955-
  Stuck in a small world : staying on board with your not-so-unique yet
thoroughly dysfunctional family / Steve Wyatt.
    p. cm.
  Includes bibliographical references.
  ISBN 978-0-7847-2111-7 (perfect bound)
  1. Family--Religious aspects--Christianity. 2. Christian life. I. Title.

BV4526.3.W93 2008
248.4--dc22

                              2007046507

  14 13 12 11 10 09 08   9 8 7 6 5 4 3 2 1

DEDICATION

Call me blessed.

For this, the final leg of my Small World voyage, God gave me Cindy, my soul mate, who taught me that true love really can happen.

He gave me Andrea, Jessica, and Josh—a loyal crew who stayed in the boat and believed in me, no matter how great the storm.

Then he gave me Emily, Libby, and Drew—a lively trio filled with energy and laughter.

And now, Darin and Joe.

And sweet Olivia, our newest passenger, who steers Grandpa like none other.

You are my joy, my Small World . . . and the reason I wrote this book.

ACKNOWLEDGMENTS

To echo novelist John Cheever, "I can't write without a reader." Reader, I acknowledge your integral partnership in this effort . . . and I thank you.

Neither could I write this book without drawing on nearly thirty years of personal experience and learning from the often painful situations of many other families. To you who have helped inform me . . . thank you.

Todd Call, a licensed marriage and family therapist in Arizona, was my right arm in this project. He ensured that the direction offered here is both biblically accurate and consistent with accepted practices in family therapy. Todd, your contribution was enormous . . . thank you!

Wanting to keep *Stuck in a Small World* abundantly *real world*, I assembled a team of researchers, who each adopted a family circumstance that best described his or her own *stuckness*. In addition to research, they also shared their personal stories—providing insight that greatly enlarged my understanding. Thank you Ron and Vickie Crowe, Susan Wyatt, Kimberly Garofolo, Eric Theis, Don Fentsermaker, Kathy Spraetz, Corrie Wilson, Mark and Joni Corby, Laura Vesely, Yvonne Gill, Gary and Cheryl Rosser, Catherine Fogerlie, Rick Wappel . . . I hope I didn't miss anybody.

Keeping me on schedule and unearthing documentation was the lot that fell to Patti Snyder and Gin Fagan. Thanks can't even begin to describe how I feel about those two.

God graciously carried me through the darkest time of my life in my Small World. Thank you, Father, for helping me process my storm so that I could share words of hope.

CONTENTS

SURVIVING LIFE IN A SMALL WORLD

On a trip to Southern California, my wife Cindy, the boys, and I decided to make the obligatory stopover at Disneyland. Realizing the boys would want to ride all the rough-and-tumble stuff, I'd already decided that I would need to temper my boyish ways and visit a few attractions suited more to Cindy's liking.

> **Little did I know the adventure lurking for me on the other side of that bridge.**

The first test of my quixotic plan came when the boys lined up to ride Space Mountain. Are you kidding? I wanted to go too! But I mustered my resolve and pointed Cindy toward Fantasyland instead. And then, even as a familiar chorus was already filling my ears, I chivalrously laid my coat beneath my bride's feet and valiantly (if somewhat reluctantly) led her across the bridge leading to (*sigh*) It's a Small World.

Little did I know the adventure lurking for me on the other side of that bridge.

The line was rather short (compared to the line for Space

Mountain), so I happily concluded that my selfless act would be rewarded with such a quick trip through Small World that I'd actually be able to "do the right thing" and still make it back in time to join the boys at Space Mountain!

We boarded our boats in record time, which was good because that song "It's a Small World" was already beating against my brain. But once we launched into the journey, I found myself actually enjoying the experience.

That's when the unthinkable happened. We got stuck in Small World!

The boats stopped. Sadly, the music did not.

Our ship had stopped right in front of the hula girls. So between the swishing grass skirts and that mind-numbing refrain, "It's a small world after all," it didn't take this reluctant visitor long to start plotting an escape: *If I can just stick my left leg over the side of the boat and shift my weight out onto that fake concrete shoreline, and if I can manage to do that without tipping the boat and drenching Cindy, then maybe I can weave my way through those grass skirts and around the volcano and those plywood palm trees. Look, there's a ladder. This is a piece of cake!*

But just as I leaned over to describe my plan to Cindy, the loudest, most obnoxious voice since Roseanne Barr's screamed over the loudspeaker: "This ride is experiencing a temporary maintenance issue. Please DO NOT EXIT YOUR BOATS! Please! Remain seated, and we will resume operation shortly."

At first, I considered making good my escape anyway, but peer pressure (and that stupid conscience of mine) got the better of me. So I sat . . . and sat. Meanwhile, the music kept playing . . . and playing. The grass skirts kept swooshing . . . and swooshing.

After about twenty minutes of that nonsense, someone at master control finally decided to the kill the song (not the skirts, just the song). And as soon as I heard that wonderful sound of silence, I found myself shouting at the top of my lungs, "Thank you!"

Cindy promptly turned twenty-seven shades of crimson and punched me in the ribs. All the other "boat people" were laughing.

That's when it hit me: *I've got a captive audience!* So . . . overgrown seventh-grader that I am, I started rocking our boat—and because all the boats are connected, all the other boats started rocking too. In fact, by the time several other immature forty-somethings had also joined in, we were splashing water all over those hula girls!

When the music started up again (not the boats, just the music), instead of groaning and praying for cotton balls from Heaven, I stood up and—with a Captain-Jack-Sparrow-like glint in my eye—said, "Here's what we're gonna do! Everybody sing 'Small World' in your own native tongue!" (If you've ever been to Disneyland, you know that plan was genius!) I even started directing my hastily assembled choir! And everybody (except Cindy) was having a blast.

I think that's when I understood: it wasn't chivalry that landed me in this predicament—this was a God thing. . . .

SMALL WORLD AS PARABLE

In the weeks prior to this getaway, I encountered several family issues involving some of the people in our church. And each predicament seemed thornier than its predecessor. I began reflecting on the families in our church, and I convinced myself that not only has the occurrence of family strife escalated these days, the enormity of the issues we face has also shot right through the roof.

I started thinking, *Doing family is harder than it's ever been! The problems people face today are so gnarly, and lately they seem to be coming at warp speed!*

I spoke with a friend who was feeling tense about an upcoming family wedding. She described some of the relational squabbles she feared might erupt. She sighed deeply and then asked, "Do you suppose *any* wedding is totally free from family dysfunction?"

Some parents in our church asked a gifted family therapist to help them sort through various teen issues. These moms and dads were thoroughly committed believers, yet each troubled family was dealing with a child who was wandering from the faith. One was hooked on meth, another was bipolar, and a third was the proverbial rebel without a cause. And for each family, life at home was a war zone.

The more I thought about the realities, the more I concluded that the human capacity for dysfunction has radically increased! We're facing bigger problems and more potentially volatile issues today than mankind has ever faced before! Why, in my city of Phoenix alone, the divorce rate has reached nearly 70 percent.

Yet something inside me said, *No, that's a bunch of hooey! The families described in the Bible were no different (certainly no better and no worse) than the families I know today. Back then, some families were loving and caring, while others were out of control and hopelessly dysfunctional. And most families, just like today, were a mix—somewhere in between.*

For each family, life at home was a war zone.

I grabbed my Bible and started researching some of Scripture's most famous heroes of the faith. And as I turned the pages on their family biographies, I began to realize that dysfunctional family life has always been with us! Even among the greatest of God's great ones there existed every type of prickly family conflict you could imagine.

That's how I later made the connection that doing family is a lot like being stuck in a Small World.

Remember the lines from that painfully repetitive song? I sure do: "It's a small world after all . . ." At Disneyland that song is meant to remind us that whether we were born in Chicago or Chile, Botswana or Boca Raton, we all are part of the same human family. And even if our skin types are different—we're talking everything from red and yellow all the way to black and white—it doesn't matter! We are precious because we really do share citizenship in a very, very small world . . . after all.

I began to realize that the stresses being felt in most homes today are not new stresses. Even *your* family stress. The one that has you crying into your pillow, racking your brain for solutions, wishing at times you could just crawl out of your boat and quietly walk away . . .

YOUR FAMILY IS NOT UNIQUE

King Solomon said: "What has been will be again, what has been done will be done again; there is nothing new under the sun" (Ecclesiastes 1:9). No matter what you're going through, it has happened before in other families.

Including, for example, doing the parent drill without a partner. I discovered for myself that single parenting isn't hard—it's *impossible*! Raising kids and managing a home takes maximum effort even with two engaged in the process; but when the responsibilities fall on only one, it becomes a monumental challenge. When the demands of raising children, the burden of providing an adequate living, *and* the job of maintaining a home are shouldered solo instead of duet (and you also throw in stuff like guilt, fear, rejection, plus a thousand other heartaches unique to the single parent), the task is almost insurmountable!

This may surprise you, but single parenting is as old as the

Bible itself. It's true. We don't even know her name, but in 1 Kings 17, a single mom was gathering sticks to build a fire so she could bake a final meal to share with her only son. She was so desperate: "We're about to eat our last bread . . . and then we're gonna die" (see v. 12).

Talk about afraid! She had no money; she had no food; and now, thoroughly defeated and utterly disenchanted, she was also flat out of hope. Thankfully, the prophet Elijah was there. He wasn't the kind of "prophet" who sells hankies, waves his hands around, and shouts, "In the name of Jehovah, don't you daaaaaare get out of that boat!" Hope was Elijah's top agenda. So he called on the Lord and took care of her food problem.

This may surprise you, but single parenting is as old as the Bible itself.

Later when her son died, Elijah urged her to do something far more stretching than just not leaving her Small World boat. He basically said, "Lady, your Small World problem is too big for you to go it alone. What you have is a God-size problem. You need to give God control of your son" (see v. 19).

Another single mom, Hagar, is highlighted in Genesis. The baby's father had decided to put Hagar out of his life. In fact, he gave Hagar a day's ration of bread and water, then sent her packing! (see Genesis 16; 21:8-14). No child support, no visitation arrangements. Abraham helped make a baby and then refused to pay for the baby he made! Sound familiar?

Maybe you're the *child* in this story. Maybe you got stuck in a one-parent home. You know what it feels like to have a parent walk away. Every day of your life you wrestle with feelings of rejection, wondering if maybe God made some

STUCK IN A SMALL WORLD

tragic mistake by giving you breath at all. That's exactly how Hagar's baby felt. And sadly, it doesn't appear as if Ishmael ever quite got over it. *Hostility* seems to be the best way to describe the legacy Ishmael handed down.

Some dissonant family songs never stop playing.

Nestled between the lines of Ishmael's sad story is something the boy himself may never have grasped, but it was nonetheless absolutely true: "God was with the boy as he grew up" (Genesis 21:20). God was intimately engaged in what was happening to him. God saw the anguish of that boy's frightened mom. He heard young Ishmael crying when he was terrified that he would die. And God came alongside to be with both of them. Ishmael may have felt alone during those painful years when his own dad walked out, but that's exactly when God walked in.

Let's fast-forward to Jacob and Esau. The twins' parents were extremely unwise in how they favored their favorites. Truth is, they were so out of balance that eventually an all-out civil war erupted in that home! The phrase *sibling rivalry* doesn't even touch it! The Bible says, "Esau held a grudge against Jacob because of the blessing his father had given him" (Genesis 27:41), a grudge that significantly altered his life.

And the truth is that, like it or not, some dissonant family songs never stop playing. Those same tired themes are repeated at every holiday, with the same old off-key chords and angry lyrics that lash out at familiar victims.

There have always been family relationships that refuse to heal, brothers who hate each other and who rip each other off . . . That stuff's not new. And sometimes just remembering that can help. It can bring you peace in knowing that although your family circumstance may never change, at least you're not the first to have to endure it.

Jacob got the blessing but not his dad's favor. You would think he had enough scars from that to bend over backwards to get it right when *his* young'uns came along. Think again. Jacob had twelve sons, but Joseph was his favorite; he even gave him a special coat. And though Joseph was much younger than the other boys, Jacob put Joseph in the position of reporting on his brothers. Eventually, Civil War II broke out. Joseph's brothers angrily sold him into slavery and then told dad that he was dead.

Genesis 39 mentions no fewer than four times that God was with Joseph (vv. 2, 3, 21, 23). God gave him protection and intervention and, ultimately, success throughout the entirety of what Joseph would no doubt describe as the most horrible period of his life. At every step along the way, God was not only there but was orchestrating the events to his own glory and to Joseph's ultimate good. Thankfully, Joseph had just enough reason to hope; so he stayed in the boat and kept rowing through some very choppy waters.

Even though Joseph could've easily blamed his mom and dad, his brothers, and even his sister for the rest of his life for . . . you name it—repressed anger, lingering bitterness, persistent anxiety, fear of rejection, a tendency toward deception, an obsessive desire for control—he didn't do that!

Isn't it good to know that others have already emerged from exactly what you are just now going through?

Instead, Joseph chose to rise above many of the same negative influences you also may have experienced. In addition, he refused to repeat his deeply entrenched family behavioral patterns. He rejected the oft-chosen path of just knuckling under to genetic predisposition, and he chose instead to do what was right.

In fact, once his family's conflict had finally come to an end, Joseph told his brothers something that I have remembered countless times as I endure my own Small World garbage. He said, "You intended to harm me, but God intended it for good" (Genesis 50:20).

Isn't it good to know that others have already emerged from exactly what you are just now going through? And while you may not enjoy being stuck there, you need to know that you're not the first. A few of those pioneers have actually left bread crumbs revealing a path, a workable guide, not for just coping but for truly rising above your circumstances.

That's what this book is about . . . after all.

Stuck in a Small World will also piece through the ancient wreckage of the life of a little baby named Moses. Talk about an ill-timed birth! In the midst of Egypt's culture of death, Moses came into the world. Can you relate? If you've also been surprised by a pregnancy—or maybe *you* were the big surprise—the pain is at times overwhelming. But listen, what others may call a mistake, God calls great.

WHAT YOU CONSIDER ILL-TIMED, GOD CALLS RIGHT ON TIME

Because Jochebed (Moses' mom) remained faithful and because Moses cultivated a relentless resolve to follow God, both mom and son have left for us some navigating directions so that we can find our purpose too. Hebrews 11:23 says, "By faith Moses' parents hid him for three months after he was born, because they saw he was no ordinary child, and they were not afraid of the king's edict."

See that? They were *not* afraid. And one of the reasons they weren't afraid is because they knew that the place where they found themselves was not unique. Too many people in *our* culture might have said, "Time out! *My* situation is different! I'm outta here, baby!" But Moses and his parents stood firm. And because they did, Israel once again survived.

David was more passionate about winning awards and climbing ladders than he was about raising godly children.

Along the way, we're also going to visit Eli, a priest whose biological children were embarrassingly carnal. They lived in the same house, but they weren't even close to being on the same page. Not spiritually.

We'll also visit David—hard-charging, highly successful David—who did *his* parenting on autopilot. And because David was more passionate about winning awards and climbing ladders than he was about raising godly children, his kids suffered dearly from his neglect. Know anybody like that today?

Talk about paying dad's tab! David's kids became embroiled in every kind of dysfunction you could imagine—from sexual misconduct all the way to murder. In fact, one of his kids, Absalom, actually set David's best friend's fields on fire! Burned 'em right to the ground!

I think Absalom was just starved for dad's attention. Maybe your kids are torching fields too. If so, David's story will uncover some powerful counsel for how you can get unstuck from what might seem to be an entirely irreversible Small World.

Did you know that even Jesus got stuck in a Small World? We don't think of him in these terms, but Jesus was the product of a blended family. His father, Joseph, was really his stepfather; and his brothers and sisters were actually half brothers and sisters. Even though Jesus was always perfect—or maybe *because* he was always perfect—he was on the receiving end of the same jealousy and abuse that many blended-family kids continue to face today.

Jesus discovered, long before *we* ever did, that most stepfamilies *don't* blend. And if you try to make them blend, things will get ugly (and somebody's gonna get creamed). But there is a better way, which I call the SWIRL effect.

Continuing our Small World voyage, we'll make another stopover in John 9 and meet a man who was blind from birth, as well as his parents, who had faithfully cared for their special-needs child. And even though he was now fully grown—"of age" as the Bible puts it in verse 23—he was still under their care. He was an adult child with special needs. Surely his mom and dad, like some of you, often wondered, *Will we ever get unstuck from our Small World?* But God has a word of hope, even for families coping with special needs. So please, don't jump ship!

Even though Jesus was always perfect—or maybe *because* he was always perfect—he was on the receiving end of the same jealousy and abuse that many blended-family kids continue to face today.

Then there's the young man so given to self-destructive behavior that he cut off all ties with his family. He lived on the streets and did what some kids are doing today: he cut himself. His extreme responses may make you think of a chemical addiction or bipolar disorder. Let's just say he was obviously dealing with some very devilish issues. The Bible tells us that he often would "cry out" (Mark 5:5). For help . . . for relief . . . for release. And he wasn't the only one in his family who was crying.

We'll end our journey with the story of the prodigal. He's

the one who packed all his bags in search of a better life. He prematurely climbed out of his Small World boat and tried his hand at making life work. In fact, he "spent everything" (Luke 15:14) in search of that elusive goal. It's in his story that you may find hope to continue living out your own story.

TIMELY TRUTHS

It's been months since my Small World epiphany, yet I'm still amazed by the profundity of what I discovered: doing family really *is* a Small World! Not only did our faith ancestors encounter more than their share of sticky family problems, the problems they faced were not much different from the ones we face.

There are two truths we're going to keep revisiting in this journey, truths I believe can help you survive your Small World.

Truth 1: No family circumstance is unique

Solomon was right: there *is* nothing new under the sun (Ecclesiastes 1:9), nothing you could ever face that hasn't already been faced—and even survived. And although it's true that your family's song is really irritating sometimes (with its constantly repeating melody and those obnoxiously self-serving lyrics), remember . . .

Truth 2: It's always too early to get off the boat

Now before we launch this ride, I want you to understand that I know a little something about wanting to get unstuck from a Small World.

When I got married the first time, it was for life. I was raised to believe (and believed so passionately) that marriage is a permanent deal, that divorce is never an option. I actually banished the D-word from my vocabulary. Not even in our worst days did I ever allow that foul word to cross these lips. *Divorced* was an ugly place I knew I would never find myself in.

And yet it happened. In spite of my every effort to the contrary and despite my firm belief in marital permanency, I became—it's still difficult to form the word—*divorced*. My wife told me she didn't love me anymore; she wasn't sure she ever did. Then she walked out on me. Not once, but twice. And not just on me; she left behind our three children as well.

Shame? I felt it in spades. And a huge chunk of my shame was because I had disappointed God's family by losing *my* family. I had convinced myself that ministers aren't supposed to face the same problems *real* people have to face. And I'd even begun to believe the lie that Christian leaders like me have somehow arrived, that we've somehow scaled to that lofty place where divorce and other such atrocities can never reach.

Today I know better. I understand that every family has "business"—even a minister's family. Yes, family is where we're supposed to be able to incubate personal conviction and gestate moral character. But there's not one home across this vast country that is absolutely issue free. Not one.

I had convinced myself that ministers aren't supposed to face the same problems *real* people have to face.

Family is where we are first confronted with somebody else's flaws—and maybe even our own—but we often have the protection and the privacy we need to work through those flaws away from the glare of public consumption. The trouble in my case was, my private family business suddenly became everybody's business. The shame I felt was beyond description. I wasn't just concerned about embarrassing

God's family; I was equally concerned about the impact my garbage would have on my extended biological family.

I started thinking a lot more clearly about my biological family. Without even knowing it, I was developing what family therapists call a genogram. A *genogram* is basically a family tree on steroids. It's a family diagram on which—in addition to names, dates, and birthplaces—there are also penciled in each person's diseases, dysfunctions, and disorders.

Was I in for a rude awakening! On one branch of my tree is a family with all but one of the kids sexually abused by their father. On another branch is a long chain of alcohol and drug abuse. Just name it—over-the-counter medications, illegal drug use, family members drying out in rehab, plus numerous charges of public drunkenness. One especially heartbreaking branch involves a young man who lived in an overtly homosexual lifestyle before taking his life with a drug overdose. Another involves a beautiful young woman, formerly married to a man, who now claims she is a lesbian.

God offers solid, hopeful counsel that can help you rewrite the music of your difficult family ordeal.

Teenage pregnancy? We got it. Family members living together outside of marriage? Got that too. Abortion? Yep. And let's not even try to track all the sexual infidelities. One part of my family has experienced divorce across the span of three generations—most of those listed on that branch have never known the security of an intact nuclear family.

But it's not just big scandal stuff. My genogram also notes a double amputee, blindness, severe chronic depression, bipolar disorder, mental retardation, panic disorders, Down syndrome, obsessive-compulsive disorder . . . and that's the short list.

My clan has known its share of relational brokenness.

STUCK IN A SMALL WORLD

On one branch, one sibling hasn't spoken to her brother in ten years. Another branch involves brothers who can't be in the same room ten minutes without shouting obscenities at each other. The dysfunction is so rampant that one family member has opted out of the family. She pretends the rest of her branch doesn't even exist.

That list is the *stuckness* of only one family. By every measure, it's a typical, all-American family. Except it's *my* family. My largely Christian family. And several players mentioned are either currently serving or used to serve in professional ministry. I understand wanting to get out of the boat! However, before you wag your head in disgust, or launch into some diatribe on the screwiness of Steve Wyatt's sorry family, run an inventory on *your* family. Go ahead. I dare you. Do a genogram on your clan.

And if your list doesn't look an awful lot like *my* list, here's the deal: I'm gonna let *you* write this book's sequel, and I'll be the first in line to buy your story. As an added incentive, I will also provide your entire clan with very attractive "I Have No Issues in My Small World" T-shirts.

My Opus

Stuck in a Small World is more than just theory for me. The two truths above have been forged on the anvil of my real life, lived out in real time while I was solidly planted right here in the real world. And because that's true, this book—shaped by the experience of someone who never imagined that *he* would ever get stuck—is chock-full of real hope.

This book is my opus, if you will, to families stuck in familiar places. More than my story, it is God's story. From Bible times, others have been stuck in exactly the same places you may be now. But God offers solid, hopeful counsel that can help you rewrite the music of your difficult family ordeal too.

While *stuck* is anything but a unique experience, it *is*

an inexplicably painful one. And downright challenging at every level. Add the grass skirts that keep swooshing to the incessant dissonance of the same refrain droning endlessly—day in and day out, month in and month out, year after year after year . . .

Meanwhile, some of your family and friends may not appear to be in the boat with you anymore. Oddly, they seem to be planted safely on the shore. *Why won't they swim out and help me?* you wonder. As they watch from relative safety while your vessel takes on water and rocks to and fro in the waves, they're content to scream instructions you already know to be true: "Stay in the boat! Do not, under any circumstances, leave your boat!"

While what they say is true—that it's *always* too early to climb out of your boat—what you long for, what you're looking for is a real-life, flesh and blood person who understands what you're going through. Someone who has already ridden out his storm—and lived to tell about it.

I believe God allowed me to experience all the personal pain my ride through Small World brought because I'm supposed to tell you (as someone who's been there) that there *is* some smooth sailing ahead.

Stuck need not be your final destination. In fact, God himself, a Father who's got a whole lot of kids in various stages of *stuck,* once made a promise on that very theme. He said, "I know the plans I have for you . . . plans to prosper you and not to harm you, plans to give you hope and a future" (Jeremiah 29:11).

The stories that follow can help lead you into the very heart of the hope-filled future God has planned for you. And hope is a God thing . . . after all.

PARENTING
WITHOUT A
PARTNER

1 Kings 17:8-24

➡ PEOPLE LIKE YOU

Christy* tried to provide money, food, clothing, and shelter for her three children ages seven, five, and two. She worried about her children and what kind of teenagers and adults they would become. She knew she was going to catch the blame for leaving their daddy, now and for years to come. She also knew that she was going to have to be the heavy, the disciplinarian. And her kids would resent that. She didn't want to have to play that role. She wanted to give them everything they asked for, a yes to every request and whim. After all, that's what they deserved. Hadn't they been through enough?

But what about *her* pain? She had already faced the fear of leaving, being on her own, and the damage that had already been done to her children. She blamed herself for not acting sooner, for letting things happen, and for putting herself and her children in the situation to begin with. She felt shame for what had happened, and her self-esteem and confidence were eroded to the point of nonexistence. She knew she was in over her head, so she decided to ask for help. She went to Salome's House, a domestic violence shelter.

* Names in all case studies in this book have been changed.

This chapter title implies a not-so-subtle subtext, because its two dominant words—in root form—share the same letters. They're mixed around a bit, but check it out: to spell *partner* you use the same letters required to spell *parent*. You can't even get started as a parent unless you have a partner. It's also hard to *succeed* as a parent without a partner.

I know that seems basic, but it's true: God has designed parenting to be accomplished as a team. The job's tough enough when you've got somebody beside you to help carry the burden—but when you've got to go it alone, it's a real Small World!

When I became divorced, I was a basket case. Divorce is brutal. Don't let anybody tell you otherwise. It's the ripping apart of a dream. Not a neat surgical incision—but a gaping, slashing tear. It's the splintering of the present, a violation of the past, and a desecration of the future. Like a pane of glass now shattered, millions of shards scatter everywhere.

After an extended period of licking my wounds and wishing I could just breathe my last and be freed from all this torture, I finally realized that life had to go on. So I said to myself, *What happened, happened. I can't change my story. Divorce is now my past, and nobody—no matter how gifted—can change the past. I'm no longer married. BUT I AM STILL A PARENT! I've got three kids who are depending on me. So if I can't find my way through this mess, they're not gonna find their way either. So stop whining and get with it! These kids need their dad—and, sad for them, you're him!*

That's when it first hit me: *I am a SINGLE parent!*

One day I stood at the trunk of my car and did something I never dreamed I'd do: I pulled out my golf bag and stored it in the garage. Single dads don't have much discretionary time, so golf was going to have to be put on hold. Not that the game would suffer much from my departure; I love golf so much I take about 20 percent more swings than most everybody I know! Still, when I pulled those clubs out of my car, it felt like part of me was dying.

Another wake-up call came when I was in the grocery store. My daughter had asked me to pick up a certain feminine product—and I thought, *I can do this!* Till I got to the place where those products are displayed. I'm not lying—they took up a whole aisle, half a football field long! We're talking light days and heavy days and overnight . . . and green bags and pink boxes and blue clover . . . and let's not even discuss wings!

It's the splintering of the present, a violation of the past, and a desecration of the future.

I called my daughter and asked, "Jess, what kind?" I paced up and down the aisle while she gave me play-by-play via my cell phone!

"What color bag?"

"Dad, it's not a bag; it's a box."

"What brand again?"

"Always."

"Jess, that's not a very good name for this stuff."

"Dad!"

"Sorry. How does it come equipped again?"

I got so engrossed in fulfilling the objective of my mission that I forgot I was on my cell—and I started talking as loudly as most obnoxious people talk on their cell phones.

"Ah, Jess, they got a deal going. A box of five hundred for three dollars. Is that all right?"

Have you ever had the feeling that somebody was watching you? Well, some guy was peeking from around the shampoo aisle and laughing his fool head off at me! I could deal with him. But there was also a little old lady with a crease in her brow, a glare in her eye, and a look on her face . . . like I was some kind of pervert or something!

I'll be honest, that's about how well it went during my years flying solo. We never did figure it out. Yet somehow, together, we made it. We came up with our own routines, we managed to keep the house fairly clean, and there were even a few days each month when we could find the laundry room. But for the most part, it was hunt and peck . . . all the way to the finish line.

A TV commercial that once ran featured a blank screen except for the question "How Much Does the World Weigh?" Nerdy science-types are tempted to pull an Arnold Horshack and say, "Ooh, ooh, ooh, Mr. Kotter! The answer is 6 sextillion, 588 quintillion tons! That's the mass of planet Earth!" But the commercial wasn't asking about our planet in that sense. It asked, "How much does the *world* weigh?" Flashing onto the screen came the answer: "Just ask a single mom."

There were times when I worried about money, but I didn't tell the kids 'cause they might have panicked too.

To you who've been there, that's how it feels. Your days aren't just full—they're crammed! Up at 5:00, full speed through the day, down for the count by 9:15. In my past life, I had toggled between *Leno* and *Letterman* with the religious fervor of an Islamic cleric! But now . . . 9:30 and I was out! We're talking grocery shopping, meal prep, bill paying, and housecleaning—and I didn't get paid for any of it!

I was mom *and* dad. Counselor *and* friend. Disciplinarian *and* chauffeur. Breadwinner *and* homemaker. Day in and day out. Week in and week out. There was never a break, not even a twenty-second time-out!

There were times when I worried about money, but I didn't

tell the kids 'cause they might have panicked too. I was worn out but didn't complain, for fear that they might think I was going to walk out too.

At first I was determined to be Superdad. I was going to do it all—and I was going to do it all perfectly. So I launched a new business, kept the house, paid the bills, did the laundry—plus whatever else it took to keep my three teenagers and me on solid ground. I even tried (unsuccessfully) to fill the void left by their missing mother. But as time passed, I became more and more frustrated, more and more exhausted, and less and less effective.

Finally, I admitted, *I can't do this perfectly. I'm not even sure I can get to mediocre! So maybe what I need to do is just do the best I can.*

Welcome to the Small World of the single parent.

Talk about *Fear Factor*! Give me a spider to eat anytime! Dangle me from an airplane, sink me in quicksand, put me on an island with Rosie O'Donnell and Donald Trump . . . But please—don't make me come home from a long day at work when there's no food, no time to go *get* food, and no money to drive through Sonic. That's real fear!

DOING LIFE IN A CRUCIBLE

I'm not the only one who has felt that impact. Let's go to the Bible, because you need to know that the single-parent experience is neither new nor is it all that unique. Let's travel all the way back to 1 Kings 17, where we find a widow and her son who were living all alone in a place called Zarephath.

Interesting name, Zarephath. It literally means "to melt." In noun form it means "crucible."[1] My definition of *crucible* (simplified from the dictionary's) is: "a container that can resist great heat for the purpose of melting metal." Zarephath wasn't exactly a weekend in Maui. This woman was living in a crucible!

It's the same address, sadly, where you or someone you know lives. You had to sell your home? Your possessions were divvied up? The kids are constantly shuttled back and forth? Then there's the discomfort of having to change your checking account, update your mail, plus bump into old friends at the mall.

And what about the crucible of worry? *Will the kids be OK while I'm at work? Can I hold us together on the pittance I make? What if he doesn't pay child support?*

And the granddaddy of them all . . . *Will I be alone for the rest of my life?*

That's Zarephath. It's a Small World whose nagging theme song is all about worry, fear, and way too many sleepless nights.

Talk about financial insecurity! This widow's Small World had been so utterly reduced that she was gathering sticks—stupid twigs—so she could cook one last meal for herself and her only son. She had just enough oil and just enough flour to bake one last loaf of bread.

Yet at that very moment of desperation, some *man*—whom she'd never even met before—showed up and asked her to help *him*!

"Would you bring me a little water . . . so I may have a drink?" (v. 10). Like . . . she didn't have enough to do already!? When you're a single parent, the *last* thing you need is somebody else wanting something.

◆ "Mom! Where's my lunch money?"
◆ "Dad! Andrea's hogging the laundry room!"
◆ "I'm hungry!"
◆ "I need cash!"

And when you're a single parent, you don't have the luxury of saying, "Go ask your father (or mother)!"

Compounding this woman's financial fright was an equally oppressive giant called sheer exhaustion. It was all she could do to cover the needs of her own family, let alone some stranger's. Of course she thought, *Get your own water, dude!* But it wasn't just water. The stranger also wanted bread. (At least he said please!) However, when she explained that she didn't have any bread, he cavalierly replied, "Go make some!" (see v. 13). Isn't that just like a man?

DON'T BE AFRAID

This woman had no way of knowing, but God had sent Elijah to help her. God knew she was destitute. He knew she had no resources. He knew there was no money in the bank, no food in the pantry, and no extended family to fall back on.

She blurted out, "As surely as the LORD your God lives, . . . I don't have any bread—only a handful of flour in a jar and a little oil in a jug. I am gathering a few sticks to take home and make a meal for myself and my son, that we may eat it— and die" (v. 12).

As soon as Elijah heard those words, *he* also knew why God had sent him. So he said to this frightened, desperate woman, "Don't be afraid" (v. 13).

When you're a single parent, the *last* thing you need is somebody else wanting something.

Then he made her a promise: "Go home and do as you have said. But first make a small cake of bread for me from what you have and bring it to me, and then make something for yourself and your son. For this is what the LORD, the God of Israel, says: 'The jar of flour will not be used up and the jug of oil will not run dry until the day the LORD gives rain on the land'" (vv. 13, 14).

When you're desperate enough and your wallet is empty enough, you'll listen to just about anybody if it means keeping your family fed! But when that voice reverberates with such confidence and with a tone of such convincing authority, you know it's from God! So she obeyed.

And sure enough, "There was food every day for Elijah and for the woman and her family. For the jar of flour was not used up and the jug of oil did not run dry, in keeping with the word of the LORD" (vv. 15, 16).

Now when you fall into a sweet deal like that, you keep it going, right? So the woman said, "Hey, prophet guy! Would you like to hang out with us till the famine's over?" So he stayed. And for the next two years, life was pretty good at Zarephath. Until the son got sick.

Nothing major at first—everybody gets sick. But he didn't get better. Instead, "he grew worse and worse, and finally stopped breathing" (v. 17).

Can you believe it? The boy died. And that's when mom absolutely lost it! She scooped her boy's dead body into her arms and asked a question every parent asks God in the face of unspeakable loss. She asked, "What do you have against me?" (v. 18).

She addressed this question to Elijah, but she was really asking it of Elijah's God. It's obvious this woman was distraught! She could hardly speak because she was choked by rage (and strangled by guilt, as we'll see in a minute).

Her angry heart probably screamed, *You call yourself a prophet! You speak in the name of the Lord? Big deal! It's true you fed us. So? All that means is, now he's gone and I'm here all alone. If that's the kind of God you serve, count me out!*

It's very natural to be disillusioned in a time of grief. When your Small World shrinks even smaller, you tend to say things that later you can't believe you said. You question God's wisdom, you doubt his love, and you even deny his goodness. The widow must have been thinking something like this: *If I had known that giving you bread*

would keep me alive—but alone—I never would have given you even one bite!

MAD AT ELIJAH AND AT HIS GOD

But it's more than anger. After "What do you have against me, man of God?" she added, "Did you come to remind me of my sin?" (v. 18).

Is that why this happened? Is this some kind of judgment from God? There is no more guilt-ridden creature in all the world than a single parent. It's like everything bad that happens is some edict from God that you blew it, that you couldn't hack it, that you should be a better provider, that your marriage didn't make it . . . which somehow makes you either incredibly flawed or morally suspect.

My middle child actually browbeat me into dating again.

One single mom said she lost it when her three-year-old asked, "We're not a family, are we, Mommy? We don't have a mom *and* dad. We just have a mom. (*Sigh.*)"

And money? When you're a single parent, you're so guilt-ridden for the harm that has already hit your kids, you can't bear to let them go without anything they think they need—even to the point of your own financial ruin. And time? You'd like to be more social. But if you go out, you feel guilty; if you stay home, you feel wronged. It's a guilt machine.

My middle child actually browbeat me into dating again. Her theme song was that she wanted me married before she left for college, just so she'd know I'd be OK. She even helped pick out the woman who today is my wife. She kept prodding till I finally asked Cindy out.

Then we got serious and decided to be married. But when I made the big announcement, that same daughter exploded into violent tears! When I asked why, she said, "Because it's not supposed to be this way, Dad! *I'm* supposed to get married, not you!"

I just wanted to die in a pile. Wiping away my own tears, I said, "I know, honey. And I'm sorry. I am *so* sorry."

Successful single parenting boils down, ultimately, to one all-powerful skill: *accepting* **the things you can't change.**

When you're a single parent, you're the only one your kids can depend on, but you're also the only one your kids can blame. You're always on pins and needles, afraid you're gonna blow it—that if you're not really careful, you might warp them somehow.

When you're divorced, you're constantly measuring the emotional damage your divorce caused them. And every time something goes wrong, you wonder, *Is God punishing me for what happened? for not being stronger? for not finding a way to somehow hold it together?* I believe something similar was tracking through this widow's mind. Every day at her son's bedside, she tried (in vain) to find a reason, some explanation for his ill health. Till finally it clicked: *God is judging me. He's taking my son because of my sin.*

FORGETTABLE . . . IN EVERY WAY

But that's not how God works! I don't care how convoluted your Small World may have become, your family's sad song was not written by God. No matter how your life story has unfolded, God isn't angry at you! And he has no plans to even the score either. If you are a Christian, in the moment you confessed your sin to God, that sin was not only forgiven; it was forever forgotten!

God "does not treat us as our sins deserve or repay us

according to our iniquities. For as high as the heavens are above the earth, so great is his love for those who fear him; as far as the east is from the west, so far has he removed our transgressions from us" (Psalm 103:10-12). When God forgives sin, he "remembers [our] sins no more" (Isaiah 43:25). Now *you* may remember. And other people will *definitely* remember. But not God. When it comes to forgiven sin, he chooses to forget.

I'm so impressed with Elijah. He didn't rebuke this woman, he didn't correct her, and he didn't even quote forty-seven Bible verses to her. He simply said, "Give me your son" (1 Kings 17:19). Elijah knew this situation was way bigger than her questions. This was a God-size problem that only God could resolve.

Elijah spoke two directives to this woman, the same two I believe God wants to speak to your heart. Remember the first thing Elijah said? "Don't be afraid" (v. 13).

He essentially said, "I know you're overwhelmed. And I know you think there's nothing left but to bake your last loaf, then curl up and die. But what you *really* need to do is stop focusing on what you *don't* have. Focus on the little bit of oil and the handful of flour that you *do* have!"

If you're stuck in this Small World too, stop beating yourself up and worrying yourself to tears over how bad you've got it or how hard the kids are taking it . . . or whatever else your worry list may include. Instead, learn this singularly valuable lesson: the key to surviving the Small World of parenting solo is acceptance.

Yes, you need to diligently change the things that you *can* change. But successful single parenting boils down, ultimately, to one all-powerful skill: *accepting* the things you can't change. And there's a lot about single parenting that you just can't change. You can't change your child's absentee parent, but you *can* change your attitude toward him or her.

You can't change your financial situation, but you *can* change how you respond to it. You can't change the fact that you've been victimized, but you *can* choose not to remain a victim.

On the other hand, you can be ticked at your ex-spouse and pull all kinds of stunts to make him pay. You can endlessly harp and harangue about being left all alone to handle the kids: ". . . and besides, *I* didn't want this divorce; he did." But if you stay that course, you'll find that fewer and fewer people are willing to listen to your harangue. They'll just flat-out get bored with hearing it. Other people don't want to hear about how you're out of bread all the time. Or how unfair your situation may be. Or how angry you are at God!

Please, let it go. I understand there's a *lot* about your life you wish you could change. But if you keep focusing on all that stuff, it will not get any better—*you* will end up getting a whole lot worse.

Doin' Life on Just One String

Nicolo Paganini was one of the most gifted violinists in the world. He also may have had a touch of David Blaine in him. The story I heard was that Paganini was once playing a difficult piece before a packed-out audience when, suddenly, a string on his violin snapped. Yet Paganini kept playing anyway, improvising magnificently. Unbelievably, a second string broke. And then a third! Now, a violin only has four strings. And three of them were dangling from Paganini's violin like a dog's tongue on a hot afternoon! Yet this courageous musician completed the composition anyway. Talk about a showman!

The audience was so amazed, they leaped to their feet and shouted, "Bravo! Bravo!" When the applause finally died down, Paganini asked them to sit down. And even though they knew there wouldn't be an encore, they sank into their seats anyway.

Paganini then held the violin high for everyone to see. He nodded to the conductor, turned to the crowd, and with a twinkle in his eye, he smiled and shouted, "Paganini . . . on one string!" Then he placed the instrument under his chin and played his final piece . . . flawlessly.

Talk about grace under pressure! "Paganini . . . on one string!"

Some people maintain that such stories of Paganini are urban legend. They don't deny that Paganini played on just one string; what they don't believe is that it was accidental. They say it was all part of the showman's shtick![2]

Regardless, here's my question: What's it gonna be for *you* when you're doing family on one string? I know all too well, playing *that* song is hard! Will you play your song with anger and bitterness? *(How unfair that my violin would dare break!)* Or will you choose forgiveness instead? Maybe you just want to give up. Will you slam your violin to the floor and stomp away in disgust? Is that your plan?

Will you keep hating those who hurt you? Or are you going to choose to live in expectant, exuberant hope and keep playing?

The widow of Zarephath decided to keep singing in her Small World. She played the song God gave her to play, even though it meant playing her song with just a handful of flour and a tiny drop of oil. All she had was one string on her instrument, yet the Bible says she did what Elijah told her to do. And sure enough, God did the rest!

Instead of whining about one last meal, she was dancing in the streets like Paganini, saying to any who would listen, "Zarephath . . . on one lump of dough! Is God great or what?"

Acceptance is the only attitude that will sustain you through your Small World. Not bitterness nor self-pity . . . and certainly not fear. But a courageous acceptance that says,

"God, if this is the song you want me to play, I'll play it—even on only one string!"

◆ "Yeah, but you don't know how I've been hurt."

◆ "You don't know the creep I was married to."

◆ "You don't know how hard it is to keep holding this all together."

No, I don't. But as one who has been in a similar place, I know that as long as you wallow in fear, you will remain . . . forever . . . a *victim*.

I didn't want to be a vict*im*. I wanted to be a vict*or*. I wanted to overcome. I was determined to rise above. And for me, the key to getting there was finding some way to accept the awful circumstance that was now my life. And to not get stuck in the boggy quicksand of a broken, fearful heart.

The second thing Elijah said to the widow was as powerful as the first. He said to this rage-filled, guilt-ridden woman, "Give me your son" (v. 19). Trouble is, she just couldn't go there, so Elijah "took him from her" (v. 19). He carefully, lovingly, and ever so gently gathered the boy into his arms, placed him on the bed, and prayed.

The key to getting there was finding some way to accept the awful circumstance that was now my life.

Then he did something that probably even took *him* by surprise. He "stretched himself out on the boy" (v. 21). Body on body, leg to leg, arm to arm, face to face. As though somehow there might be a transfer. That maybe the warmth of his body could bring warmth back to that boy's body. Then he did it again. And again.

This is the first time the Bible mentions that anyone had ever been raised from the dead. So Elijah couldn't review his lecture notes from Prophet's Institute for a quick refresher!

I believe Elijah did what he did because God told him to. Then he prayed, "O LORD my God, let this boy's life return to him!" (v. 21). And guess what? That boy started breathing. God raised him to life again!

Then Elijah took him to his mom and said, "Look, your son is alive!" (v. 23). And that's when it clicked! That's when this woman finally understood what her Small World journey had been all about. She said, "Now I know that you are a man of God and that the word of the LORD . . . is the truth" (v. 24).

GOD IS THE PARTNER

It wasn't just her son's resurrection that convinced this woman. I mean, we'd *all* get it by then! No, it was the whole scene. Every single snapshot, every vignette, every encounter . . . every shading and every subtle wrinkle in this story.

It was God sending someone so she wouldn't have to keep doing the parent drill alone. It was God strangely refilling the flour jar when, hours before, it was empty. It was God somehow finding a way—at times dramatically, at other times unobtrusively—always meeting a need, providing an answer, and sending a helper.

I wish every story ended that way. But they don't. My story didn't include any miraculous resurrections. Oh, we had our moments. Tiny cracks in an otherwise impenetrable wall. Hairline fractures that let in just enough light so I could see my way through another otherwise dreary day. Moments when my kids would do something off the charts just to express their love for me. Moments when a financial need would be met in a way I never imagined and never tried to manufacture. Moments when family or friends came along—unbeknownst to them, at absolutely crucial moments—and they helped me.

These moments didn't happen daily, but they *did* happen.

And sometimes it seemed as though God would wait for the last possible minute before he came through—but he always came through! And every single time, I was reminded that God was tracking my every step—and that my Small World wasn't so small after all. Because God himself was partnering with me in the parenting of my children.

Nearly every day of my journey, the words of Psalm 68:5, 6 sustained me. There David described our God as "a father to the fatherless" and a "God [who] sets the lonely in families." He provides a home, a place of belonging, to those who are lonely.

Sometimes it seemed as though God would wait for the last possible minute before he came through.

You *don't* have to go it alone. God himself has promised to be a Father to your fatherless children. He's promised a safe place for those who are lonely and so afraid. And when you finally choose to believe that—when you receive the words of Elijah and decide, *I'm not gonna be afraid anymore*—and when you release your death grip on your kids, when you stop assuming full responsibility for everything that happens to them, you invite God to work.

When you give your children into the safekeeping of their heavenly Father, you'll witness a kind of resurrection. It's a whole new way of living! Because you finally realize, *I'm not flying solo after all! And he is an exceedingly more wonderful partner than I could ever have had in some mere human. I have the Father God of the universe parenting beside me, directing me and protecting my kids.*

For the follower of Jesus Christ, there is no such thing as a single parent. There is not now, nor will there ever be, just one string on your instrument.

So play your song. And as you play, remember the two things Elijah said:

Don't be afraid

Your God is watching over you. When you need something—and I mean *really* need it—he'll send someone to help you. He will provide for your every need. I know, because he said he would. And he did it for me.

Give God your children

You've got to release your brood into his safekeeping. He already has his perfect way marked out for them. And he has also promised to be a Father to them.

Triggering this release can feel extremely scary, but here's how it happened for me: In the very instant I made my release, I experienced an indescribable, unimaginable relief absolutely flooding across my heart. My eyes were opened to resources, strength, and support from people and places I never could have imagined on my own.

I don't know how he does it—but I've seen it happen. And I believe it can happen to you too. I can't tell you what you may have to go through to get there. Neither can I tell you exactly how God will help see you through—but I *can* tell you that he brought me through!

Looking back, I know now there was never a day—not even one single minute—when I was alone. So keep your head up . . . and keep your heart strong. Stop living in fear, and quit clinging to your kids.

Instead, with a confident courage in your heart, hand your tribe over to God, a partner who fathers the fatherless. They're his kids too . . . after all!

CONCEIVED IN CHAOS

Genesis 16:1-16; 17:15-22; 21:8-21

➡ PEOPLE LIKE YOU

Robert was seven when his dad died. The day of the funeral, still in denial, he hid under the table and watched the feet of the strangers in his home go by. In the following eight years, he gradually progressed into drug and alcohol use, unbounded random sex, destructive relationships, and other out-of-control emotions and behaviors at home and at school.

His mom was dealing with her own grief and loss issues, but they never talked about it after she took the pictures down. Robert eventually wound up in a treatment program after his mom realized she could not handle his behavior anymore.

There has been massive research on the effects of a single-parent home on children. The odds are stacked against them. They are more susceptible to peer pressure, sexual promiscuity, struggles with emotions and relationships, and using or abusing alcohol and drugs. Without intervention, these problems can last a lifetime.

Our society is full of adults who were lost as children and still have not found their way. Perhaps the largest and most controversial body of research pertains to fatherless homes. Children growing up without a father seem to experience the struggles listed above more acutely than children without a mother. Single fathers tend to remarry at a higher rate than single mothers. The benefits gained from having a father and a mother, biological or not, are vital to the future identity formation and relationships of the child as he grows.

God understands that we need some flesh and blood people who once experienced what we are now experiencing—and who found their way through. That's why he has candidly dealt with Small World issues from the beginning of time. You think single parenting, parental neglect, deadbeat dads, and broken homes are new deals?

Wrong. They're as old as dirt.

A Single Parent and a Princess

A single parent is mentioned in the first book of the Bible. Her name was Hagar. She had come from Egypt with Abraham and Sarah to serve as Sarah's personal attendant. She was fleeing the vile corruption of her homeland and was probably glad to attach to Abraham and Sarah because they seemed like good people. But you never know who people really are until you live with them.

Hagar didn't leave Egypt to become a surrogate mom. She had no plans for becoming Abraham's part-time lover. The poor girl just wanted a job. But somehow, things got twisted.

Have you ever expected life to go in one direction, but it ended up going an entirely different direction instead? Things didn't start out messed up, but that's how they turned out. Hagar didn't choose this story line. Sarah did. Sarah's name means "princess." And her name fit. Sarah was a tad high maintenance. Not a bad person, she just found a way to always get whatever she wanted.

For one, Sarah married a really rich dude named Abraham. For another, she and her hubby had received an amazing promise from God. God had told them that he was giving Abraham a lush new land that Abraham and his descendants would possess—forever. He also promised that Abraham would become the founding father of a new nation called Israel.

Now that's pretty cool, but don't forget the other part of the story. Abraham had married a princess—so whatever Princess wanted, Princess got. The story of Abraham, Sarah, and Hagar tells us not only about the first single parent but also about the first separation, the first case of what most of us today would consider an extramarital affair (even if the culture of the day allowed men to go against God's plan of having one wife), *and* the drama endured by the first child born into such a mess. The part that *really* intrigues me is how God dealt with that mess.

Although Abraham and Sarah loved each other, they couldn't have children. That's a sad reality for any couple, but in Abraham's day it was a disgrace. (Almost as shameful as not owning your own cell phone is in our day!) It was a disgrace to Sarah because barrenness was considered a curse from God. And it was devastating to Abraham because he was rich but had nobody to whom he could leave all that money.

God had promised a child, that he would open Sarah's womb and give them a son, but then he made them wait for a *really* long time. We understand this waiting period as a test of faith, but Abraham and Sarah didn't—so they became very impatient. After all, they were getting on in years. Abraham was seventy-five when God first gave this promise, and Sarah's biological clock had stopped ticking decades before that.

So Abraham and Sarah decided to help God out. Actually, not *they*. Princess Sarah dreamed it up. Abraham just went along with it, and you'll soon see why. Sarah decided that since she was barren, Abraham should make a baby with her maid Hagar (Genesis 16:2). And since Hagar was a slave and had no rights, they could keep her baby and . . . voilà! God's promise would be fulfilled!

Surrogate moms were common back then. They didn't use

artificial insemination. If my wife said, "Honey, I want you to have sex with this beautiful young thing who works for me!" I'd be looking under the couch for Ashton "You just got punk'd!" Kutcher! Yet there's probably not a man alive who doesn't understand to some degree why Abraham replied, "That's a really good idea!"

Sure enough, Hagar got pregnant. And that's when she also got prideful! What woman doesn't get that part of the deal? Hagar really rubbed it in: "I'm carrying your husband's baby!" She no doubt wore tight clothing so her bulging profile would be right out there. She munched on crackers with her mouth open. She took lots of bathroom breaks and even propped her feet up to watch *Oprah*! She was so in your face that, finally, Sarah blew her cork! She even got in Abraham's face and criticized him for the aftermath of this hare-brained scheme! (see v. 5).

Uh-uh! Abraham didn't cook this meal; Sarah did! Granted, it didn't take much to convince him, but this was Sarah's stupid plan. Yet Princess got so mad, she twisted the facts and blamed him for this fine mess.

A Stuck Man

Like most men Abraham was clueless. "Honey, Peaches, Sugar-Doll . . . I only did what I thought you wanted me to do! How come I'm knee-deep in doo-doo?" How come? Because sex is more than just a physical act. Sex isn't merely biology; it's a bonding. And you cannot bond with someone without bonding *to* that someone. Abraham loved Sarah. But there was another attachment now, plus that little zygote floating inside Hagar's belly.

Talk about conceived in chaos! Hagar's little baby had no idea that his new family was such a mess—his fertilized egg was about to be booted out of the family before he even got hatched! Hagar's baby didn't get to choose his situation.

Nobody gets to. You just start moving toward that strange, new light—and then, when you finally break through, somebody swats you on the bottom! You look at mom, then you look at dear old dad . . . and start screaming like a banshee!

Even though Sarah and Hagar were once quite close (how else could Sarah have conceived this idea?), along with Hagar's bulging belly came a growing hostility. Finally, Sarah wanted Hagar *out*! Like most men who enjoy being clueless, Abraham washed his hands of the whole deal. Still, you can't help feeling sorry for the guy—there's nothing worse than being caught between two women who despise each other. It's hard enough when it's your mom and your wife you're trying to please. But can you imagine this scene? No wonder he told Sarah, "Do with her whatever you think best" (v. 6).

What Sarah thought "best" was a severe thumping around Hagar's head and shoulders. In fact, she so mistreated Hagar, the Bible says Hagar ran for the desert to hide. Can you imagine how that woman must've felt? Her shape had been forever altered, her financial circumstances were suddenly in the toilet, and even more she was now all alone.

Not so long ago, Hagar was the apple of Abraham's eye; now she was scorned. She was the winner of a prize she'd never get to claim, the secret passion of a powerful man; now she was in exile. All because she was having a baby, a baby we don't talk about much.

Like most men Abraham was clueless.

Poor kid. He was the sad consequence of a hasty (and extremely foolish) decision—and nobody seemed to see him as a real person. He was just a pawn in everybody else's plan. He was an inconvenience, and both he and his mommy were in desperate straits because of it.

God was really moved by this predicament. After all, Hagar was no threat to Sarah. Sarah was beautiful. And rich. Not to mention, Abraham's wife. And it was painfully obvious Abraham would never see Hagar as anything more than a baby factory, just a convenient mechanism for helping God fulfill the promise.

Hagar was born a slave, and she would die a slave. And if she had stayed in Abraham's house, she would have died serving a woman who hated her guts.

But remember God's promise, that he is "a father to the fatherless"? (Psalm 68:5). "The angel of the LORD found Hagar near a spring in the desert" (Genesis 16:7). The verse doesn't say *an* angel of the Lord. It's *the* angel of the Lord. This is the first of several Old Testament references to the angel of the Lord (1 Kings 19:3-9 being another example). Many scholars believe these are pre-incarnate manifestations of Jesus.

God is a *good* husband. He knew Hagar needed to talk.

I realize that's a mouthful. But here was Hagar, everybody's nobody, yet Jesus himself "found" her, which obviously means he'd been looking for her! Then having found her, he gently spoke to her heart. If you feel like Hagar right now, Jesus knows exactly where you are. And he wants to come alongside and sit with you too!

Wow. He *found* Hagar. He didn't wait for Hagar to find him. And he didn't even wait for her to ask him to come to her. He just came! And then he asked a very probing question: "Hagar . . . where have you come from, and where are you going?" (Genesis 16:8).

That's a question husbands *seldom* ask. It's like asking your wife, "How was *your* day?" Most men don't ask open-ended questions, primarily because our wives will happily answer!

> Over the last 15 years, a series of books and articles have told us that women talk a lot more than men do. According to Dr. Scott Halzman in *Psychology Today*, women use about 7,000 words a day, and men use about 2,000. On the other hand, Ruth E. Masters, in her book *Counseling Criminal Justice Offenders*, tells us that "Females use an estimated 25,000 words per day and males use an estimated 12,000 words per day." And according to James Dobson's book *Love for a Lifetime*, research tells us that "God gives a woman 50,000 words a day, while her husband only gets 25,000."[1]

Pick your poison on which expert is correct; but no matter which stats you choose, it's obvious that men are done talking (and therefore, through listening) long before their counterparts even get warmed up!

But God is a *good* husband. He knew Hagar needed to talk. Who else could she talk to? All alone . . . in the desert. Truth be told, her whole life has been spent alone.

The Lord asked a question that framed Hagar's deepest heartache: "Tell me, Hagar. Where have you been? And where is life taking you?" (see Genesis 16:8). Trouble was, being a slave, Hagar wasn't used to people listening to her. She could only speak when spoken to, and then very briefly and to the point. So she just blurted it out: "I'm running away from my mistress" (v. 8).

That's when the Lord told Hagar to do something that sounded like anything *but* a good plan. He said, "Go back to your mistress and submit to her" (v. 9). God will always tell you what you *need* to hear but not necessarily what you *want* to hear. And yet, if Hagar had kept running, her life would've become a dreadful misery. After all, she was pregnant, and this was the desert!

She was carrying Abraham's only child, and he had all the financial resources to hunt her down and bring her belly back. Once brought back, she would've been severely punished. And even if she *did* escape, she would've spent her whole life raising a fatherless child. Because she was a slave, he too would be a slave. But if she went back, as God instructed, her baby would have a shot at a better life than hers had been. A much better life.

Her choices weren't ideal, but Hagar's obvious and best choice was to go back. Sensing her fear, the Lord added this encouraging promise: "I will so increase your descendants that they will be too numerous to count" (v. 10). Imagine what that must've meant to Hagar! "If you do this," God was saying, "I'll give you your own family—children to care for you and even some grandbabies you can spoil!"

Then came the cherry on the sundae: "You . . . will give birth to a son. You are to name him Ishmael, for the Lord has heard about your misery" (v. 11, *NLT*). Hagar obviously knew she was pregnant. But to find out she was having a boy was great news because Abraham wanted a boy! Bearing him a son would mean everything to him!

God's compassion grabbed her heart even more. My view is that Hagar had never had anyone care to know her so intimately; and beyond knowing her, who cared for her so deeply. Surely she wondered, *Who is this God who would speak to someone like me?* Her gods were from Egypt. But what had they ever done for her? She prayed to them, but they never answered. *This* God took the initiative to find her; then he spoke to her and reassured her! For the first time in her life, Hagar thought, *I really matter!*

But Hagar's new God also told her something she *didn't* want to know. He told her what her little boy would be like. "He will be a wild donkey of a man [*say what?*]; his hand will be against everyone and everyone's hand against him, and he will live in hostility toward all his brothers" (v. 12). Ishmael's tag fit too. "He's gonna be a handful, Hagar!" Now that's hard news, but at least she got a heads-up!

Hagar was so touched by God's kindness, she even named her new God. "'You are the God who sees me,' for she said, 'I have now seen the One who sees me'" (v. 13). Somebody had finally paid attention to that overlooked, underappreciated slave girl. Someone finally took the time to listen to her, and that somebody was the Creator of the universe. And not only was *she* in his care, so was her unborn child.

Maybe, like Hagar, you're parenting without a partner. Or you're living in daily anxiety concerning the financial welfare of your family. Maybe the future (as you see it) feels *terribly* frightening. If so, follow closely because our God never changes. He's the same today as he was in Hagar's day (see Hebrews 13:8). The blessings Hagar received are the same blessings God wants you to receive too.

GOD'S PURPOSES FULFILLED

Hagar returned to Sarah and, not long after, gave birth to a bouncing baby boy. As God promised, the baby was named Ishmael. And boy, did Abraham *love* that kid! In fact, for the next thirteen years, Abraham believed that Ishmael was his heir, *the* heir, to all of God's promises. But that's not how it came down.

Instead, when Ishmael was thirteen years old, God told Abraham, "As for [Sarah] your wife, . . . I will bless her and will surely give you a son by her. I will bless her so that she will be the mother of nations; kings of peoples will come from her.' Abraham fell facedown; he laughed and said to himself, 'Will a son be born to a man a hundred years old? Will Sarah bear a child at the age of ninety?' And Abraham said to God, 'If only Ishmael might live under your blessing!'" (Genesis 17:15-18).

Abraham loved Ishmael so much, he was perfectly fine with leaving *him* his estate: "I don't need to go through this daddy drill again; I'm fine with giving Ishmael the inheritance. It doesn't matter whether he's Sarah's son or not. He's *my* firstborn. And I love him! Let's just bless *him*!"

God agreed to bless Ishmael, but not as Abraham expected. God said, "I'll bless Ishmael. But Sarah will still bear a son, and you'll call him Isaac. I will establish my covenant with him. As for Ishmael, I've heard you. I will surely bless him. I'll make him fruitful and will greatly increase his numbers. He'll be the father of twelve rulers, and I'll make him into a great nation. But my covenant I will establish with Isaac" (see vv. 19-21).

A year later Isaac was born. And when he became a toddler, Abraham threw a party for him. However, sometime during the party Princess got ticked off—again. She overheard some attitude from Ishmael—the Bible says he was "mocking" (21:9), no doubt precious Isaac. He probably was just making fun of his dopey little half brother 'cause that's what big brothers do! Except Ishmael was a total donkey, remember? So he might've even been roughing the kid up a bit—we just don't know.

God gave a green light to a very less-than-ideal family separation because sometimes God has a purpose in brokenness.

When you're ninety years old and you've waited twenty years to finally have your own kid, of course you'll overprotect and overreact. Princess did both. She took one look at her baby and at this teenage thug—then pulled Abraham aside and read him the riot act: "Get rid of that slave woman and her son, for that slave woman's son will never share in the inheritance with my son Isaac" (v. 10).

Now time out! Wasn't Ishmael Abraham's son too? And wasn't Abraham the rich half of this dynamic duo? Yet Princess said, "That kid isn't getting any of *my* money!" And since you can't argue with a princess, Abraham was in a pickle. So God pulled him aside and said, "Do not be so distressed about the boy and your maidservant. Listen to whatever Sarah tells you, because it is through Isaac that your offspring will be reckoned. I will make the son of the maidservant into a nation also, because he is your offspring" (vv. 12, 13).

God was not affirming Sarah's plan because Sarah was right in what she said. No, God gave a green light to a very less-than-ideal family separation because sometimes God has a purpose in brokenness.

God's ultimate purpose can't be shut down—even in the worst thing that ever happened to you:

◆ When your daddy walked out on you, or maybe he stayed but never talked to you—all he did was neglect you.
◆ When your grandma raised you because mama refused.
◆ When you had to move to a strange new place.

Ephesians 1:11 says that God "works out everything in conformity with the purpose of his will." He works out *every*thing. Even broken things. Including *your* thing . . . and Abraham's too. ("Abraham, I know telling your son good-bye will hurt, but I still have a purpose.")

Since that's true . . . think maybe it's time *you* stopped weeping over the wouldacouldashouldas in your life? Think maybe it's time for you to stop whining about who didn't love you, who wasn't there for you, and who didn't come through for you? Listen, God has you right where he wants you. And there is *nothing* that he's ever allowed to happen to you that doesn't first square with the purpose of his greater plan for you.

Of course Ishmael should've been able to joke around with his baby brother without getting kicked out of the family! But God had a purpose.

Did Abraham care that he lost his son? Of course. This decision that God affirmed as right sure didn't seem right for everybody. It wasn't right for Abraham, it wasn't right for Hagar, and it wasn't right for Ishmael. Only Princess appeared to benefit. But God had a purpose.

So "early the next morning Abraham took some food and a skin of water and gave them to Hagar. He . . . then sent her off with the boy. She went on her way and wandered in the desert" (Genesis 21:14). Hold your horses! God told Abraham to send her away, but he didn't say to send her away broke. Abraham was a multi-gazillionaire! Yet all he gave Hagar and his own son were a box of Triscuits and some Fiji water!

If the family's screwy relationships hadn't damaged Ishmael enough, this drill was the final straw. It would've been hard, but these two could've made it without Abraham. There's no way they could make it without food.

If you're the Abraham in this story, if you had enough time to make a baby, make enough room in your wallet to pay for the baby you made. Maybe you can't change mistakes from your past. But you can make sure that child of yours has the resources he needs to have a decent life.

"When the water in the skin was gone, [Hagar] put the boy under one of the bushes. Then she went off and sat down nearby, about a bowshot away, for she thought, 'I cannot watch the boy die.' And as she sat there nearby, she began to sob" (vv. 15, 16).

STUCK IN A SMALL WORLD

I hate to have to say this, but all single-parent children are damaged by the experience. I know you'd like to believe otherwise—that somehow your enormous love will magically erase every potential heartache and gloss over every perceivable scar. But it doesn't work that way. The truth is, your kids will probably *never* fully heal from the damage. That's the bad news.

But I've also got some good news: that damage *can* be overcome in the same way a person overcomes any other kind of disability. Plan A is the best way to go, as mom and dad parent together from beginning to end. But Plan B can work, primarily because our God has volunteered to be a father to the fatherless.

Plan B for Ishmael included a pretty good life, but he was left with the ugly scar of an angry spirit. Even before Ishmael was born, God told Hagar how hostile he would become, that he'd do war with everybody. In other words, Ishmael would have anger issues. Now that you know his story, you understand why!

◆ When he was fifteen, he and his mom were *both* turned away by his daddy!

◆ The only dad he'd ever known went AWOL. Nobody prepared Ishmael for that.

◆ One day he was the firstborn son, heir to a vast fortune, prince of a new nation. The next day he was a homeless kid.

◆ Beyond that, Ishmael had lived in a home where his mama was constantly degraded by her boss, Princess.

◆ He felt the sting of abuse as well. Sarah didn't even call him by name. She referred to him in the third person, "that slave woman's son." Can you imagine how that must have impacted him?

◆ And to be sent into the desert to die by a father who says he loves you? What kind of scar would that leave?

I believe Ishmael never healed from that trauma, that he remained an angry man. Yet in spite of his scars, Ishmael became a great man anyway. God blessed him in so many ways.

GOD IS NEAR

Ishmael was blessed even back in that awful desert. There "God heard the boy crying, and the angel of God called to Hagar from heaven and said to her, 'What is the matter, Hagar? Do not be afraid; God has heard the boy crying as he lies there. Lift the boy up and take him by the hand, for I will make him into a great nation.' Then God opened her eyes and she saw a well of water. So she went and filled the skin with water and gave the boy a drink" (vv. 17-19).

During those painful teen years when dad walked out, God walked in.

Track Ishmael's story, and it's amazing! God was always right in the middle of the action! He "found Hagar" (16:7). He saw Hagar (see v. 13), meaning he understood her. And now, he "heard the boy crying" (21:17) as he lay dying. He even asked, "What is the matter?" (v. 17). And then he opened Hagar's eyes (see v. 19).

But the greatest blessing of all? "God was with the boy as he grew up" (v. 20). He stayed *forever* planted right beside that kid *all the way* into adulthood!

Our God is a God who gets involved. He saw this fatherless child and heard the cries of a single mother—and having found them, God came alongside to be with them. Ishmael may have felt alone. Even rejected. But God was with him. During those painful teen years when dad walked out, God walked in. When Ishmael's throat was parched, when it was time to take a trade and find a wife and make his own way, God was with him!

In that same way, God has always been with you too! Psalm 34:18 promises, "The LORD is close to the brokenhearted and saves those who are crushed in spirit." God not only knows all about your scars; he was with you as you received those scars.

A friend wrote me concerning that very truth:

> Steve, from the age of three until I reached seven, my aunt would take me to the country where she met the man she was having an affair with. She and her guy would drink and have sex in the car . . . right in front of me. They told me to take a nap, but I never could.
>
> I was soooooo frightened!
>
> I would just lay there, my tears puddling on that hot, sticky vinyl seat. I'd squeeze my eyes so tight and try to fill my mind with anything but what was happening right in front of me.
>
> You have no idea the peace it gives me to know that I wasn't alone in that back seat! . . . Just knowing that God was with me, crying every tear with me, was so freeing, so comforting.

That's the healing grace of an always-present God. Just knowing that there is never a time when he is not near should comfort your soul. And because God was with Ishmael and his mother, the cry Hagar couldn't bear to hear was the very call God had come to hear.

If that's true, why did Ishmael become such an angry person? Ishmael could have tapped into a more positive view. He could've rejoiced in God's presence and blessing. But instead, Ishmael chose to keep wrestling against

Abraham's absence and his lack of blessing. And because he chose that view, the anger in Ishmael's heart became a scab that he kept picking and poking at until, in time, it became an ugly scar.

That same thing can happen to you. God is always with you—and his presence is far more reliable and powerful than the presence anyone else could ever provide. But if you choose to keep picking at your wounds, God will let you. He didn't force Ishmael to get his emotions under wraps—and he won't force you either.

Ishmael enjoyed the love and attention of a doting father for thirteen years. Then when God took over the child-rearing responsibilities, Ishmael went from having a good dad to having the best Dad! His mama was so faithful, even finding him a bee-yoo-tiful Egyptian wife who gave him a whole slew of kiddos so he could love them the way he always wished he would've been loved. Not only that, he became so stinking rich that twelve of his sons became princes over their very own kingdoms!

Those countries are known today as the Arab nations, and those who live there are direct descendants of Abraham through Ishmael. And while it's true that the descendants of Isaac were the inheritors of Israel and all God's wonderful *spiritual* blessings, Ishmael's offspring got the oil. Are you hearing me? They got the oil! So God's promise is true! Fact is, God is *still* blessing Ishmael's children even to this day.

If you're a single parent or if you were at one time a single parent—and you know what it's like to do this job alone—I hope you watched as God worked in the lives of Ishmael and Hagar. In the same way God cared for them, he wants to care for you. If you'll let him, God will meet every need in your life *and* your kids' lives, just as he did with Ishmael. The hurt will be healed, and only the scars—just like Jesus' scars—will remain as a forever testimony to God's faithfulness.

Did Ishmael's scars affect his life? Of course. God told Hagar they would. But did those scars ruin his life? No, even though he kept picking and poking at those painful wounds. And the scars your children have experienced don't have to ruin their lives either. God will be with you as you teach, train, and care for your children. And he will be with them as they grow safely into adulthood. This season is a journey for you, a wilderness journey. And though it seems like you're all alone, you're not.

Because God is who God is, no follower ever parents without a partner.

Because God is who God is, no follower ever parents without a partner. God is with you, and he'll see to it that you make it all the way through. Your child will experience many things. He'll know fear, confusion, and yes, anger. He may even act out a bit because he's got all kinds of emotions raging inside and he doesn't feel like he has control over any of them. But remember, God is with him too. And he's going to stay with him. So don't be afraid. God is faithful. And he's promised to be with you.

If you're an Ishmael, if you know what it feels like to have a parent walk away, here is a word of hope: I do get some of your pain because I've watched my own Ishmaels deal with theirs. I've sat by my son's bed and listened to his anguish. I've held my angry daughter and absorbed every blow because her heart was so confused, no words could adequately express it.

Please remember what we learned in chapter 1: although you *cannot* change what has happened to you, you *can* change how you respond to what has happened to you. And just as for Ishmael, God can take what seems to be utter disaster and what someone else may have intended as harm, and he can use it to make you strong! If God could take a kid *this* close to death—because of his father's irresponsibility and his stepmom's relentless cruelty—trust me, he can bless your life too.

The truth is, none of us comes from a completely ideal situation, even those who did have two parents. Life, being what it is, tends to knock all of us around. There's not an adult alive who couldn't show you his or her scars. Yet our God can mend every tear, span every breach, and fill every hole.

You must make a choice. Like Ishmael, you can be angry—for the rest of your life, if that's what you choose. But there are consequences. Genesis 25:18 says that the immediate descendants of Ishmael "lived in hostility toward all their brothers." You have to wonder what things might be like for the descendants of Ishmael in the Middle East today if Ishmael, four thousand years ago, had really clung to the God who stuck by him and protected him during all his troubles.

Please . . . don't remain in spiritual chaos. Your kids deserve better than that. And God has a better life for you than that. Let the healing begin. Your life to this point is what it is; you can't change it. But you *can* open your eyes and see that God gave you something to drink even while you're trekking through your desert. And you *can* look around and remember so many times when he's protected you and been with you. Why not give thanks that although everybody else in your life may walk away, God never will. He'll make sense out of the chaos . . . after all.

HE NEVER HEARD THE WORDS

Genesis 25:20-34; 27:1-43

➥ PEOPLE LIKE YOU

Chris and Traci were sisters two years apart. The rivalry was heated; it was a competition for mom's affection and dad's approval. Since Chris was older, Traci wanted *her* attention and favor too. She did not get it. Instead, she received the abuse of an older sister and the codependent leanings of an emotionally broken-down mother. Both girls were lost in a world of teenage pressures of every kind. One minute they were bosom buddies trying to navigate teenagerdom together, the next minute fighting each other for survival and for the scraps of relationship left in the family. Their story has a happy ending. But it got worse before it got better.

Children are resilient. However, they cannot stand up to the emotional and mental games parents sometimes play with each other or with their own children. Children are not pawns to be used against another parent or family member, yet it does happen. Favoritism is felt more than heard—oftentimes much more by the ones who are not the favored. The upshot of the whole thing is that in the end, the child who was favored will not respect the parent who favored him or her. The tables have been turned. Now the child, who for so long sought the approval and acceptance of the parent who favored him, is the one from whom approval is being sought.

The family we started tracking last time, Abraham's family, has more twists than a Bavarian pretzel. And even though Abraham was called "God's friend" (James 2:23), and even though the Bible describes Abraham as "the father of all who believe" (Romans 4:11), the family of Abraham was a total train wreck.

Talk about stuck in a Small World! Abraham's family song reflected a world of hardly any laughter, a world of a whole lot of tears . . . and not much hope either, but a wide, wide world of fears. There was dysfunction on every branch of Abraham's family tree.

Remember the whole Hagar deal? Isaac's dad slept with another woman, made a baby with her, and then brought that woman *and* her baby to live under the same roof with his legal wife and his "legitimate" son! And no, things didn't go so well. Even though it had been Sarah's idea (after all), she got *so* honked off that she booted Hagar and her son, Ishmael, right out of the house!

Almost from day one, mankind's definition of *family* already included in-laws and outlaws, stepkids and half brothers, mistresses and parental neglect, infidelity . . . and yes, verbal if not even physical abuse. And there was no Dr. Phil who would ask, "How's that working for you, Abe?"

We followed Ishmael's trail in the last chapter. In this chapter, we'll check out Abraham's other son, the favored one. Yet as we peek behind the tent flaps of Isaac's family, we'll soon discover that his family story is just more of the same.

Isaac's Branch

Isaac was forty years old when he married Rebekah. And even though he was getting frumpy, he married a woman who was drop-dead gorgeous! However, Rebekah was barren. She and Isaac wanted to have babies, but they couldn't.

Sound familiar? Thankfully, Isaac refused to follow in the footsteps of his father. Having lived through that mess, Isaac, now facing this same problem of infertility, must have made a promise to himself: *I will* not *repeat the bad choices of my father!* So instead of manufacturing his own solution, "Isaac prayed to the LORD on behalf of his wife, because she was barren" (Genesis 25:21). He didn't run off with some substitute woman in a hare-brained scheme to help God out. No! He prayed.

Isn't it ironic how those of us who felt stuck while growing up in a Small World (primarily because of the stupid choices and foolish sins of our parents) often turn around and make the very same mistakes and commit the very same sins they did? Your mom got pregnant by her teenage boyfriend, and your life was really hard because of it. Yet what are you doing? Sleeping with your boyfriend. Or your dad had an alcohol problem. And whenever he came home drunk, stuff got broken. Shouting matches ensued. And not even your pillow could soak up all those frightened tears. But of course, *you* don't have a problem . . . or do you?

While there is an environmental factor in why people behave as they do (for example, often those who abuse have been abused), it doesn't have to determine the whole story. But if you're not careful, you can allow your environment to become an excuse.

Isaac broke his family chain. He refused to play the role assigned to him by his dysfunctional family. Instead, he prayed. And sure enough, "The LORD answered his prayer, and his wife Rebekah became pregnant" (v. 21). With twins, no less. Twins that "jostled each other within her" (v. 22). Many translations say they "struggled" with each other. *The Message* says they "kicked."

Whatever was happening inside Rebekah, it wasn't fun and games. We're sure because she asked the Lord, "Why is this happening to me? [*I'm a first-time mama. Maybe this is normal. But with these two sluggers? My womb feels like Yankee Stadium!*]" (v. 22).

God said, "Two nations are in your womb, and two peoples from within you will be separated; one people will be stronger than the other, and the older will serve the younger" (v. 23).

SPORTS CARS AND SPATULAS

In other words, the conflict already underway inside Rebekah would continue. Through Jacob would come the Israelites, through Esau the Edomites. This family feud was just beginning.

Sure enough, "When the time came for her to give birth, there were twin boys in her womb. The first to come out was red, and his whole body was like a hairy garment; so they named him [...*Elmo? No*...] Esau" (vv. 24, 25).

"After this, his brother came out, with his hand grasping Esau's heel; so he was named Jacob" (v. 26). By the way, *Jacob* means "trickster." We'll soon see that his name fit too.

Verse 27 tells us one of two key factors why this nuclear family ended up going *really* nuclear! It says, "Esau became a skillful hunter, a man of the open fields" (*NLT*). Picture a belly-scratchin', 'bakky-chewin', gun-totin', F-250-lifted-pickup-drivin' man's man! Think Larry the Cable Guy! Add a big hairy chest, back, and arms—plus an appetite for wild game—and you've got Esau. Hey, not only could Esau kill his own food, he grilled it too! Slay it, fillet it, buffet it! That was Esau's motto.

Meanwhile, Jacob was Esau's total opposite. He "liked to stay at home" (*NLT*). Let's not go too far with this, but I picture Jacob watching HGTV and spending much of his time helping his mom tidy up the tent.

Could one set of twins be any more different? Esau sported a pair of six-guns with his initials carved in each handle.

Jacob might have had matching spatulas and an apron that read "You stab it, I'll slab it!"

Twins, but nowhere *near* identical.

PARENTS CHOOSING SIDES

The second key (and the real reason) this family imploded is disclosed in verse 28: "Isaac, who had a taste for wild game, loved Esau, but Rebekah loved Jacob."

Uh-oh. Evidently, Isaac saw himself in Esau. Rugged outdoorsman, living off the land . . . that was Isaac back in the day. And since Esau liked the same stuff Isaac liked, there was a natural affinity, which is understandable. But once Isaac allowed his affinity for Esau to become *favoritism* toward Esau, he crossed a line.

In fact, both parents crossed it. Evidently, Rebekah liked Jacob best—probably because hubby liked Esau. Plus Jacob spent more time at home.

Now just because these boys were *so* different doesn't mean one was better than the other. They were just different! However, the spark that lit the family fire was that Isaac and Rebekah chose sides. Parental favoritism is what blew this family to smithereens.

> Once Isaac allowed his affinity for Esau to become *favoritism* toward Esau, he crossed a line.

Initially, Isaac no doubt *tried* to steer Jacob toward more outdoorsy pursuits. He had to at least attempt to make him into a carbon copy of himself. That's what parents do! Just like the dad who wants his son to play football, but Justin likes piano . . . or the mom who enjoys scrapbooking, yet little Katy enjoys playing with cars . . . Evidently, after trying to make Jacob change, Isaac ultimately just dismissed the kid.

Do you understand, parent, how dangerous it is to expect your kids to be just like you? They're not!

◆ One kid is quietly creative, the other quite aggressive.

◆ One is bookwormish, the other athletically inclined.

◆ Some are naturally confident, others struggling with self-doubt.

◆ Some are happy-go-lucky, others somewhat introverted.

Why the gap? Because God has created each child to be his own unique person!

Isaac loved Esau. Rebekah loved Jacob. And both boys got damaged in the process. But especially Esau, who wasted his life acting out his disappointment, primarily because he never heard the words of blessing he so longed to hear.

Let's look at some of the resulting damage.

"Once when Jacob was cooking some stew [*true to form*], Esau [*also true to form*] came in from the open country, famished. He said to Jacob, 'Quick, let me have some of that red stew! [*What is it with this kid and red? Red hair. Red complexion. Red food.*] I'm famished!'

"Jacob replied, 'First sell me your birthright'" (25:29-31).

This deal was *so* wrong for Esau to even consider—especially given what was at stake.

I'm telling you, this kid was an operator. Jacob was always working the angles, always trying to cut a sweet deal. "Give me your birthright . . . and you can have a bowl."

Talk about a lousy trade! Usually it's the older kid who tricks the younger into stupid trades. "I'll trade you this used sweatband for that candy bar. How can you say no? Michael Jordan wore this sweatband! I swear! He did!"

"'Look, I am about to die,' Esau said. 'What good is the birthright to me [*if I'm dead*]?'" (v. 32). He wasn't *that* hungry.

And if he was that hungry, why didn't he just grab some sheep jerky or open a tub of goat yogurt? Teenage boys aren't discriminating eaters; they're garbage disposals! They eat out of cans, drink milk from the jug, eat cereal right out of the box . . . There's the pantry. Help yourself!

This deal was *so* wrong for Esau to even consider—especially given what was at stake. In those days, the birthright was an amazing privilege usually reserved for the oldest child. If you got the birthright, you'd get . . .

◆ double the inheritance the other kids got.
◆ the privilege of carrying on the family name.
◆ the right to become the family patriarch once daddy died.
◆ the blessing of a special prophetic promise from dad just before he died.
◆ the chance to be part of the lineage through which Jesus would come (well, in *this* case, because this family was all about awaiting the coming of Messiah).

And Esau was actually toying with trading in *that* level of blessing?

Granted, Jacob smelled fishy too. He took complete advantage of his impulsive big brother during a moment of obvious weakness. After all, hadn't God already said (v. 23) that Jacob would end up ruling over Esau? It's a done deal! Why was Jacob being such a jerk about it?

"'Swear to me first.' So [Esau] swore an oath to him, selling his birthright to Jacob" (v. 33).

What a bozo! He traded away millions of dollars, land, his family name, *and* the bloodline of Jesus—for a bowl of chunky soup? Check that. Magnanimous Jacob also threw in *one* whole slice of bread because he was such a great guy!

Esau "ate and drank, and . . . despised his birthright" (v. 34).

He didn't just eat soup. He basically said, "I don't care about my family heritage. I don't care if Jesus is coming!

I don't care if I don't get Daddy's inheritance. Or whether he prays over me and blesses me someday. I'm hungry *now*, and nothin' else matters!"

Some scholars claim Jacob *deceived* his brother in order to get the birthright. But there's no deception here. (That's in the next story.) This deal is straight up. It's true Jacob was devilishly shrewd. He was manipulative and definitely a greedy opportunist. But he didn't lie.

As soon as Esau swore that oath, he not only gave away his birthright but also gave away the blessing.

Esau was so impulsive he *despised* an eternally significant blessing by momentarily satisfying a passing physical need. He traded his birthright to fill his tummy. No wonder Hebrews 12:16 calls Esau "profane" (*KJV*).

As we fast-forward to Genesis 27, we change story lines. In chapter 25, we focused on Esau's cavalier approach to his birthright. But in chapter 27 it's not about birthright; it's about the blessing.

"When Isaac was old and his eyes were so weak that he could no longer see, he called for Esau his older [*and favorite*] son" (27:1).

Isaac told Esau, "I am now an old man and don't know the day of my death" (v. 2). Now Isaac wouldn't die for another eighty years! But when parts start breaking down, you wonder, don't you? You can't see like you used to. You've got a bad knee—sometimes just getting out of the car can be a chore . . . "Now then, get your weapons—your quiver and bow—and go . . . hunt some wild game for me. [*You know, the kind of meat us manly men eat?*] Prepare me the kind of tasty food I like and bring it to me to eat, so that I may give you my blessing before I die" (vv. 3, 4).

Now this blessing wasn't just wishful thinking. It was a prophetic promise, a God-inspired look into the future. However, as we saw earlier, God had already prophesied that Jacob would be the son of his promise—not Esau.

Because God already said so *and* because Esau had frittered away his birthright, by all rights Isaac should have been blessing Jacob. The blessing and the birthright were tied together, two sides of the same coin. As soon as Esau swore that oath, he not only gave away his birthright but also gave away the blessing.

However, both dad and favorite son were now conspiring against both God and least favorite son. And Isaac knew he was doing wrong. The blessing was supposed to be a huge family event, much like a wedding is today; but he was sneaking around, putting together a secret master plan. Remember, Esau was daddy's favorite! So in sending Esau out to hunt, Isaac set into motion a plot thickened by division, deception, and ultimately, destruction.

MEANWHILE, MAMA HAS A PLAN

"Rebekah was listening as Isaac spoke to his son Esau" (v. 5). Of course she was. What a family! While dad was pulling his stunt, thinking he was being so clever, mama was just outside the tent and listening in the whole time! I mean, if Jacob had issues—which he did—it's no wonder! So "when Esau left for the open country to hunt game . . . Rebekah said to her son, Jacob . . ." (vv. 5, 6).

Time out. Verse 5 says, "Isaac spoke to his son." Verse 6 says, "Rebekah said to her son." Wow! These parents don't even *try* to hide it!

Rebekah said, "Look, I overheard your father say to your brother Esau, 'Bring me some game and prepare me some tasty food to eat, so that I may give you my blessing in the presence of the LORD before I die.' [*You know what that means: your father is planning to bless Esau, not you.*] Now, my son, listen carefully and do what I tell you" (vv. 6-8).

Jacob was in his mid-forties. Yet his mama said, "Do what I tell you"? Something had definitely gone wrong with this relationship. There was a mutual clinging, an extremely unhealthy dependency between these two.

When you confess the sin you still plan to do, what you're actually saying is, "I hope I don't get caught."

When I was five and my mom gave me a paddleball, I think she was in cahoots with the toy company. That ball and rubber band fell off within twenty-four hours of purchase. Essentially that means I lost my toy, but Mom gained a weapon! The weapon worked when I was five, but one time Mom came after me with that thing when I was thirteen. Not quite the same effect. I shouldn't have, but I laughed. Even after she hit me, I was still laughing.

And if Mom came after me with that same paddle today, I'd say, "Mom, did you forget to take your meds?" *I love you, Mom, but don't tell me what to do!*

Jacob didn't have a healthy relationship with his dad, so mama was all he had. To maintain a secure place in his home, Jacob's survival plan was simple: never say no to mama!

It's possible he thought, *Mama, if God promised you, when I was still in your belly, that I would be the son of his promise, why do we have to pull a stunt in order to get me the blessing? Why don't we just let God work things out?*

But even if he did think it, Jacob was already in too deep. So he continued his family's conspiracy of silence, responding (at least, in his own mind) exactly as Adam Sandler did in the movie *The Waterboy: Mama said . . . M-mama said . . . my m-mama said Esau's the debil!*

M-mama said, "Go out to the flock [*since you don't hunt, just go to the freezer*] and bring me two choice young goats, so I can prepare some tasty food for your father, just the way he likes it. Then take it to your father to eat, so that he may give you his blessing before he dies" (vv. 9, 10).

Can you imagine? M-mama's plan was, "Let's trick the old man!" What a woman!

Jacob said, "But my brother Esau is a hairy man, and I'm a man with smooth skin. [*Esau's as hairy as Chewbacca, and I'm a walking Abercrombie ad. His skin looks like jerky, and I never go outside without SPF 4000 slathered over my tender skin. So M-mama . . .*] What if my father touches me? I would appear to be tricking him [*Appear? Did Jacob just say appear? Einstein, you are tricking him!*] and would bring down a curse on myself rather than a blessing" (vv. 11, 12).

What a great illustration of the difference between confession and repentance!

When Jacob acknowledged that this was wrong and implied, "What will happen if we get caught?" he wasn't repenting—he was confessing. A lot of people confess their sin without ever truly repenting of their sin. Jacob acknowledged that what he was about to do was both despicable and disgusting. I'd like to have asked him, "So Jacob, are you gonna stop?"

"I didn't say *that!* I'm just worried about the fallout. I'm gonna *do* it. I'm just concerned, that's all."

And *that's* the difference between confession and repentance. When you confess the sin you still plan to do, what you're actually saying is, "I hope I don't get caught." But repentance agrees that the thing you want to do is wrong— so you stop, drop, and stroll (in the opposite direction). You live not according to your desires but, rather, according to God's will.

Jacob's problem was that he was experiencing conviction

(he sensed this was wrong), and he was expressing confession (he agreed it was wrong); but he had no repentance . . . because he was still planning to *do* wrong!

So he asked his m-mama: "How can we avoid ugly consequences by being even sneakier so I don't get caught? How can we sin better?" That was Jacob's concern.

M-mama said, "My son, let the curse fall on me. Just do what I say; go and get [those goats] for me" (v. 13). She might as well have said, "Don't bother with what God's telling you to do; just do what *I* say."

And that's exactly what Jacob did! "He . . . brought [the goats] to his mother, and she prepared some tasty food, just the way his father liked it" (v. 14). Wow! They were tricking a blind guy! "Then Rebekah took the best clothes of Esau . . . and put them on . . . Jacob" (v. 15).

Sorry, time out again. When you're in your forties and mama is still dressing you, you got more problems than pasty skin!

"She also covered his hands and the smooth part of his neck with the goatskins" (v. 16). Jacob's brother was one hairy dude!

I was in Texas and went to a Dallas Mavericks game. During halftime, they held a Hairiest Guy Contest. The top five finalists were marched out to mid-court, topless, amidst the *ewwws* and *ughs* of the entire arena. We voted by applause. And the winner? Forget shaving that back; that gorilla had to *mow*! He was so thrilled at winning, he jumped down and tried to hug the cheerleaders. But with *that* mange, that wasn't gonna happen! Guess what the grand prize was? A free laser session!

Esau may have been a man's man, but he wasn't a ladies' man. He was one fuzzy wuzzy. That's why mama had to put extra fur on Jacob.

"Then she handed to her son Jacob the tasty food and

the bread she had made" (v. 17). She probably said, "Now, go trick Daddy. You smell like your brother, and you feel like your brother. Daddy's blind . . . this is a piece o' cake, son!"

Jacob went to his father and said, "I am Esau your firstborn." So in addition to deceiving his dad, he was now lying to him. "I have done as you told me [*lie number two*]. Please sit up and eat some of my game [*lie number three*] so that you may give me your blessing" (v. 19).

Well, Isaac may have been blind, but he wasn't stupid. So Isaac asked, "How did you find it so quickly?"

"'The LORD your God gave me success,' [Jacob] replied" (v. 20). Uh-huh, we've now spiraled into blasphemy! *"Praise the Lord, Daddy! I didn't have to climb a deer stand or spray urine on my boots. I just walked out and . . . thank you, Jesus! We got meat!"*

"Then Isaac said to Jacob, 'Come near so I can touch you, my son, to know whether you really are my son Esau or not.'

"Jacob went close to his father Isaac, who touched him and said, 'The voice is the voice of Jacob, but the hands are . . . [*vintage*] Esau.' He did not recognize him, for his hands were hairy like those of his brother Esau; so he blessed him" (vv. 21-23).

The trick worked. It actually worked.

"'Are you really my son Esau?' he asked.

"'I am,' [Jacob] replied.

"Then he said, 'My son, bring me some of your game to eat, so that I may give you my blessing.'

"Jacob brought it to him and he ate; and he brought some wine and he drank. Then his father Isaac said to him, 'Come here, my son, and kiss me.'

"So he went to him and kissed him. When Isaac caught the smell of his clothes, he blessed him and said, 'Ah, the smell of my son is like the smell of a field that the LORD has blessed. May God give you of heaven's dew and of earth's richness—an abundance of grain and new wine. May nations serve you and peoples bow down to you. Be lord over your brothers, and may the sons of your mother bow down to you. May those who curse you be cursed and those who bless you be blessed'" (vv. 24-29).

Again, this wasn't wishful thinking; it was a prophetic promise. Isaac thought he was giving it to Esau, but Jacob had tricked Isaac into giving *him* the blessing, something God had already promised that he would receive.

Esau returned from hunting, fired up the grill, and cooked yet another tasty treat. But when he brought it to daddy, Isaac realized he'd been duped and "trembled violently" (v. 33). Basically, he had a panic attack.

Have you ever tried to reinterpret past hurtful events by reshaping the story so you appear to be 100 percent victim?

And when Esau realized that the blessing intended for him had gone to Jacob instead, "he burst out with a loud and bitter cry and said . . . , 'Bless me—me too, my father!'" (v. 34).

But that blessing would never come to be. There was only one blessing per family. And that blessing now belonged to Jacob.

"Esau said, 'Isn't he rightly named Jacob? . . . [*Manipulative jerk! This is the second time he has taken advantage of me.*] He took my birthright, and now he's taken my blessing!'" (v. 36).

Jacob really behaved like a dirty, rotten scoundrel. But he didn't deceive Esau in round one. Round one was a clean deal. This second time *was* deception, but wasn't deception exactly what Esau was *also* trying to do? To hurry up and get the blessing God had clearly promised to Jacob?

Have you ever tried to reinterpret past hurtful events by reshaping the story so you appear to be 100 percent victim? That's Esau's complaint: "Somebody did this to me!" No, you were stupid. You did something really dumb. You shouldn't have, but you did. And now you're trying to blame somebody else for tricking you? Come on.

Now here comes a manly scene for you. "'Do you have only one blessing, my father? Bless me too, my father!' Then Esau wept aloud" (v. 38). Esau crying like a baby! Weeping simply because Jacob was a better sinner than he was. Esau totally created this problem. Had he never traded away his birthright, he might never have lost the blessing. But he did. And even though he had no one to blame but himself, "Esau held a grudge against Jacob" (v. 41) that is still reverberating today from the pages of Scripture.

LEARNING FROM HISTORY

This broken, dysfunctional family had issues! Although Jacob and Esau eventually reconciled (Genesis 32, 33), deep emotional wounds are tough to heal. There are three key takeaways in this account.

Truth 1: Parental favoritism has its perks but exacts a heavy price

Isaac and Rebekah's foolish favoritism had a damaging effect on their family and led to years of conflict between their two boys—both of whom must have struggled with perpetual insecurity. Especially Esau. Sure, he was in hog heaven whenever dad grinned and slapped him on the back because of his latest, greatest kill. But every time mama went gaga over Jacob's goat potpie, Esau boiled on the inside!

Jacob was deeply affected by his parents' dysfunction as

well. It's so sad. Middle-aged Jacob couldn't even tell his mama no! And since dad was totally into Esau, Jacob had to play his role at home in order to maintain some semblance of security!

Now what generally happens—and it happened here—is that as the kids grow up, they think this favoritism is because "something's wrong with me," rather than accurately recognizing it's mom and dad who have the problem. So the kids get angry at each other. The kids keep hoping to please their parents, trying in vain to earn that rare smile of approval—till finally, like Esau, they realize they're never going to get that blessing.

It's perfectly natural to be drawn to one of your kids more than the others. It may be an almost unconscious connection: *I don't even have to* try *with this kid! Things just work.*

As a result, you're tempted to pour every free moment into your star/starlet because you get such a big parental payback, right? Or you do special favors or go easy on discipline or express less criticism than you do with the others. But don't fool yourself; your kids are keenly aware of what's happening. You're far more transparent than you think you are. Like bloodhounds, your kids pick up even the slightest scent of parental prejudice. And if they can't see you consciously working to overcome that natural affinity, your whole family will pay a price.

Like bloodhounds, your kids pick up even the slightest scent of parental prejudice.

I read about a woman who, as a youngster, cut off her sister's hair simply because their father absolutely loved it. "The truth is," she explained, "my father was enchanted with everything about her. He was never enchanted with me."

Her eyes flooded with tears. "I can't believe it still hurts," she said.

It *does* still hurt. Such is the legacy of all children who have to witness the glow in their parents' eyes, knowing that the glow will never be focused on them.

Truth 2: Sibling rivalry isn't just mom and dad's problem

Don't label Jacob and Esau's bad behavior solely as the sad result of bad parenting. God told Rebekah before those boys were even born that they'd be a handful. Jacob was grabbing Esau's heel—trying to pull him back so Jacob could be born first—even as they were sliding down the birth canal.

Sure, your mom and dad made mistakes, but don't dump the whole guilt load on them. Esau made his own mistakes. He agreed to a really stupid deal—and lost both his birthright *and* his blessing.

So even if you did have a prejudiced parent . . . or a dad with a drinking problem . . . or a mom with a hot temper . . . God won't let you blame *them* for the person *you* have become. The Bible puts the blame for Esau squarely on Esau: "See that no one is . . . godless like Esau, who for a single meal sold his inheritance rights as the oldest son" (Hebrews 12:16).

Too many people put way too much responsibility for their own screwups on what my kids used to call their "parentals." Yet the Bible says, "The one who sins is the one who dies. The child will not be punished for the parent's sins, and the parent will not be punished for the child's sins. Righteous people will be rewarded for their own goodness, and wicked people will be punished for their own wickedness" (Ezekiel 18:20, *NLT*).

My family of origin was far from perfect. Then again, so am I. I can't just blame Mom and Dad for what I myself have chosen to do. My choices aren't their fault. If you're still trying to blame your parents for your weaknesses, you're *never* gonna break your family's chain. Never.

Truth 3: You don't have to play the role your family assigned you

You *can*—and you *must*—break your family's dysfunctional chain! Maybe like Jacob and Esau, you're the kid who got labeled. Your family's dysfunctional style used distortions and lies and even shame to create for you the role you were selected to play. As a result, you played that role of the bad child, the stupid child, the rejected child, or maybe even the unwanted child.

My point is, you can rewrite that story! Even more, you *need* to! You need to learn to see yourself through God's eyes—not with eyes clouded by sin and deception—for that's when your sense of worth and healthy identity can fully be restored.

Maybe, like Esau, you didn't get the blessing either. You weren't the favored one in your household. Well, you can't force your parents to love you like they loved her—or treat you with the respect they showed him. I really wish I could rewind your tape and make the past different for you, but I can't. That train already left the station.

But I can encourage you to do what you *can* do:

◆ Stop obsessing over the favoritism.
◆ Learn to accept the relationship for what it was.
◆ Try to make the best of it.
◆ Do whatever it takes to get over the fact that perhaps one or both of your parents did play favorites.

OK, maybe you didn't get the blessing. I'm sorry. But unless you want to pass dysfunction on to your kids, you need to get over it. And the good news is that you can! Isaac broke *his* family chain! When Rebekah couldn't get

STUCK IN A SMALL WORLD

78

pregnant, Isaac didn't score with a stranger as his father had done. He prayed, and God answered his prayer.

So it *can* happen! You *can* break the family chain!

On the downside, the chain Isaac *didn't* break was favoritism. He lived on the happy side of that fence when he was a kid. He was the favorite; Ishmael was the problem. Perhaps that's why Isaac never saw favoritism as a big enough problem to later address in his own family.

If you're still trying to blame your parents for your weaknesses, you're *never* gonna break your family's chain.

He also failed to break the chain of deception that began with Abraham. Remember how Abraham lied—twice—to save his own neck by claiming Sarah was his sister? (Genesis 12:13; 20:2). And how Isaac continued the chain by trying to sneak the blessing to Esau even though God had clearly chosen Jacob? By my count, Isaac went 1–3 on the chain-breaking scoreboard . . . proving that, yes, it *can* be done, but it's still hard.

Thankfully, Jacob's son Joseph, himself the product of severe family dysfunction *and* favoritism, would finally break his family's chain. Daddy didn't, but Joseph did.

One final word for every parent flirting with showing favoritism: unless you want your Small World to be filled with an obnoxious soundtrack marked by whining, complaining, and contention, you need to fight your natural affinity toward one child. You need to see *all* your kids the way God sees them—each as a child of inestimable value and worth.

Perhaps your parenting job was completed years ago, yet you know this is an area where you blew it. Maybe it's time to say so, to pull your grown kids aside—both "the blessed" and "the unblessed"—and tell them. Of course, they already know. But it could help them heal to know that *you* know.

And if you're the child who didn't get the blessing, it's time for you to author a new story—a better and true one. God knows you fully, yet he loves you completely. You are of such value to him that he gave his own Son just so he could save you.

So rewrite your story. And as you write, release the anger boiling within you over stuff done to you years ago. All that suppressed anger is harming you. It pops up in destructive ways like hypertension, migraines, and panic attacks. Or maybe the resentment over the way you were treated by people who didn't love you pops out—and you hurt people you *do* love. Then you wonder, *How come nobody wants to hang out with me?* All this happens because you keep trying to hide your anger rather than just write it out of your life.

Esau spent many years of his life angry—wandering about and estranged from his family. Then when someone *did* come into his life, he almost always found a way to mess it up.

The Bible says, "Anger resides in the lap of fools" (Ecclesiastes 7:9). Please don't be a fool. Stop suppressing your anger and, instead, fully acknowledge it. Then let it go. Even if you didn't hear the words you wanted to hear. Grab a pen and rewrite God's new story for your life! Isn't it way past time to start breaking that ugly chain . . . after all?

HOW TO
BE RIGHT
WHEN
WRONGED

Genesis 37–40; 41:50-52

➡ PEOPLE LIKE YOU

Joe was a young boy when it all started. And there was nothing he could do about it. He wasn't big enough or strong enough or smart enough to outwit his father, Charles, who was insecure and believed his own life to be a failure. So naturally Charles passed his insecurity along to his son. Either that or his son was going to be perfect, but at a painful price. He wanted his son to have all the things he didn't have and be the success that he wasn't. But then again, Charles *didn't* want his son to have those things. That would mean his son was better than he was, and his ego wouldn't stand for that.

Joe survived those years and had the physical, emotional, and mental scars to prove it. Later in life he was able to overcome them and find his own way despite dad's desire to bring him down. He did it with the help of many people, a determination to be different, and a realization that his past need not define who he was; nor did it have to be the shackle that held him back.

I'm currently putting together a pitch to CBS for its next installment of the *Survivor* series. *Survivor*'s producer, Mark Burnett, has drawn some intriguing battle lines between his various tribesmen and tribeswomen. Throughout the seasons (fifteen as I'm writing this), Burnett has taken on fairly dicey social controversies such as gender, class, and even the race card. What Mark *hasn't* had the guts to tackle is the family unit. I'm not talking about the Richard Dawson kissy-face type of family contest, where two families are pitted against each other in a feud to the finish. I'm talking about *one* family split into at least two—and maybe even more—rival tribes.

That's my *Survivor* plot. Split one family—unless you can find one already split—and then sit back and watch those two warring tribes duke it out until a single family member is left standing. And in *my* game, forget hauling all that expensive equipment to the Australian Outback or even the Pearl Islands. No, for my show just unpack your camera and point it at practically any home in America! Pick a house and say, "Action!" Because there is no more rugged terrain anywhere across this vast globe than inside the four walls of almost any family's home where they're trying to make life work.

Talk about a grueling challenge. My show, no doubt, will be an instant sensation as it exposes the single most difficult scenario ever attempted by man, requiring a challenge that will demand the utmost skill and cunning in order to prevail. You want to talk "Outwit. Outplay. Outlast"? Forget Cook Islands; that's child's play! This is *Survivor XVI: Stuck in a Small World*!

I'm so excited about this project. In fact, I've already completed casting for the entire show. And you're really gonna like who I've picked; it's a family we've come to know quite well already.

Abraham was the key patriarch of this clan. And even though he was called "God's friend" (James 2:23), Abraham's home life was something of a disaster. He fathered a child with his wife's personal assistant, then brought both Hagar and her son into the same tent with Abraham's wife and her "legitimate" son, Isaac.

I suppose I could've chosen *that* split for my show, but I wanted a few more cast members in order to make the story line really sing. So I kept reading. I discovered that Isaac, when he became a man, married Rebekah; and they had twin sons, Jacob and Esau. We looked at their ugly split in the last chapter.

But still, the cast was rather smallish, so I kept reading. And that's when I came to the part where Jacob—the younger of the twins—ended up marrying sisters. (Any guesses as to how *that* worked out?)

Because we don't have twelve episodes to get through this, let me quickly introduce our contestants. First, there is the tribe of Leah, which was named after a woman so homely her face could stop a clock. Not only that, she was the wife Jacob never really wanted and was actually tricked into marrying.

On the upside, Leah and her handmaid gave birth to eight boys. So the tribe of Leah consisted of eight of the ten older brothers of Joseph. For the sake of time, and because their names don't matter much anyway, we'll not even go there.

Then there's the tribe of Rachel. Rachel was Leah's little sister. And you guessed it . . . as cute as a button and the only woman Jacob ever loved. However, Rachel—though extremely attractive—was not nearly as fertile as big sister. In fact, by the time our story begins, her only son of age was Joseph. Little Ben was just a toddler at the time, and since Joseph was the obvious beneficiary of daddy's favor . . . Joseph was a one-man tribe doing battle against a ten-man tribe (counting the two brothers from his mama's handmaid).

But don't feel *too* sorry for him. There's a reason Joseph was in a tribe all by his lonesome: Joseph was daddy's favorite. He was the firstborn of the only wife daddy truly loved . . . after all. So he didn't even have to win a reward challenge; he got loaded up with all kinds of goodies that the other brothers didn't get—and he got them simply because of his DNA!

For example, without having done anything other than just being born, Joseph was given a special coat. It's often been called the coat of many colors, but it was more than that. It was a sign of nobility, a mark of favor and blessing. Giving this coat to Joseph would be like buying designer jeans for one of your kids and K-Mart jeans for the other. Or giving one of your brood a BMW Z4 coupe when he turns sixteen, and the other only a ten-speed bike.

That's just fanning the flames of sibling rivalry. And mark it down: if you do that, your kids will *definitely* split into opposing tribes. Just like Joseph and his brothers did.

There's another reward Joseph received. Even though he was the youngest of the eleven, daddy picked Joseph to be the supervisor over his brothers as they slaved in the fields. Can you imagine how well that went over? There they were, sweating it out, doing all the heavy lifting. Meanwhile, daddy's "little love child" stood—hands to the hips, coat flapping in the breeze—watching their every move!

He was the firstborn of the only wife daddy truly loved.

Joseph didn't handle all that special treatment as well as he should have. For one thing, Joseph wore that stupid coat . . . all the time. He's in the desert! What's he need with a coat? It's one thing to *get* a gift like that—but to rub everybody's nose in it by wearing it even while doing farm work . . . No wonder Joseph's brothers "hated him and could not speak a kind word to him" (Genesis 37:4).

On top of that, God gave Joseph two dreams, and both portrayed the older boys as one day bowing before Joseph. The dreams would, in fact, come true; but why did Joseph have to brag about it? Joseph told his big brothers everything. And the Bible says, "They hated him all the more" (Genesis 37:8). Of course they did!

So there you have it. Joseph's father was a self-involved, favored deceiver who continued the family chain by favoring one child more than the others. His two moms were so starved for daddy's attention, they acted like those girls on *The Bachelor.* Can you imagine? They tried to out-baby each other in a silly Who Can Have the Most Kids? competition. They were consumed with an "I'm more loved than you are!" mentality.

So where did that leave the kids? Like contestants on *Survivor,* the hurting brothers began vying for affection and scrambling for attention. All they wanted was to be noticed and affirmed—and loved. But finding none of those things, the entire tribe of Leah called for an immunity challenge.

It happened one day when daddy sent Joseph to see how the other boys were doing in the fields. His brothers saw him from a distance . . . and you probably can guess how. That blasted coat! It always gave him away—and just the sight of that thing made their blood boil. So the brothers took a quick vote. They wanted Joseph gone. The problem is, you can vote people off an island but you can't vote people out of your family! You can ignore 'em. You can pretend they don't exist. You can do your best to make their lives miserable. But you *cannot* make them go away!

So the brothers decided to sell Joseph to some traders headed for Egypt. Then they dipped his coat into goat's blood, took it to daddy, and said, "Father! (*sniff*) Something terrible happened! See the coat? Looks like Joseph bought the farm!" (*chuckle*)

"Did you say something, boys?"

"No Daddy, just choked up, that's all." (*smirk*)

So from that moment on, Joseph was no longer living at home. Yet he was still very much stuck in a Small World! See, *stuck* is all about the fallout that happens to you simply because what never should've happened in your family . . . happened in your family.

VOTED OFF THE ISLAND

Joseph was taken to Egypt and sold as a slave to a guy named Potiphar. However, even in slavery, the Bible says, "the LORD was with Joseph" (39:2). And because God was with him, everything Joseph touched turned to gold.

Potiphar, a careful businessman, kept his eyes on the books and soon realized, *This kid's a Midas!* So he gave Joseph even more responsibility until, finally, Joseph was in charge of everything!

Mrs. Potiphar had been keeping her eyes on something too, but not the books. She had been watching how good Joseph looked in his *Survivor: Small World* attire. Joseph was quite the looker. So . . . like many *Survivor* contestants, Mrs. Potiphar decided to get her groove on.

She made her move, but Joseph put her off. Then she made another move—still no response. In fact, the Bible says that "day after day" (v. 10) she came on to him. Now Joseph was no slab of marble! He was a normal, mid-twenties, hormone-charged young buck! Yet he kept saying, "No. What you want to do is wrong."

Finally, Mrs. Potiphar was through talking. So she grabbed Joseph by the coat and said, "Come to bed with me!" (v. 12). Real subtle, Mrs. P. But Joseph, determined to do right, ran right out of his coat (literally) and into the street . . . in his skivvies!

I'm amazed at the faithfulness of Joseph. I mean, "God, if there was ever a time to reward somebody—it's now! This guy said no, even though he had every reason to say yes. Do him proud, God!" But the reward didn't happen. Instead, to cover her tracks Mrs. Potiphar had Joseph's forgotten coat, and on that shred of circumstantial evidence, she falsely accused Joseph of rape.

Forget rewarded; Joseph got tossed into the slammer instead. Now remember, all this happened because of people Joseph called family. All this pain had come his way because his blood did him terribly wrong.

Joseph was in the pokey. Yet believe it or not—and I'm not convinced Joseph believed it—the Bible says that the Lord was still with Joseph (see v. 21). We know it's true, because Joseph became yet another great success—even in jail! So much so, the other prisoners looked to him as their leader. In fact, one night two new prisoners, the king's baker and the king's cupbearer, showed up. We don't know what they did to get into such trouble, but while doing their time, both of them had dreams.

"God, if there was ever a time to reward somebody—it's now!"

The baker's dream had to do with bakery stuff, and the cupbearer's dream was all about wine. Both suspected the dreams had significance, but they couldn't figure them out. So they approached Joseph. With God's help, Joseph gave them their interpretations—one a disastrous prediction (no more cookies for this baker), the other a happy conclusion (the cupbearer would get his job back).

So as the cupbearer danced out of the dungeon, Joseph

said, "Hey dude, I want out of here too! So let's form an alliance. I helped you . . . you help me! Remember me when you get out of here, all right?" (see 40:14).

"Got it!"

There was just one problem—the cupbearer was just like most survivors: "I'm not here to win friends. I'm here to *win!*"

The cupbearer decided *not* to help Joseph. He probably thought, *I've already had one bad tribal council—I gotta watch my own back! And this golden boy? He's too good. I need him out of the game!* So he conveniently forgot his promise, and Joseph rotted in jail for two more years.

The other-than-the-facts of life are often the very tools God chooses to use to help get us unstuck from our Small World!

A few years ago, the home of actress Drew Barrymore and her then husband, Tom Green, burned to the ground. Both escaped injury, having been awakened in the nick of time by their dog, Flossie. In a brief interview immediately after the fire, a reporter asked, "Are you OK?"

"Oh yeah. We're great," Drew said.

But Tom added, "Other than the fact that THE HOUSE BURNED DOWN. OH NO!"[1]

That's probably how Joseph felt.

"How ya doing, Joseph?"

"I'm doing fine . . .

◆ other than the fact that I'm in prison right now!"

◆ other than the fact that I was falsely convicted of rape!"

◆ other than the fact my that brothers sold me as a slave!"

◆ other than the fact that someone I helped refused to help me!"

◆ other than all *that*! Thanks for asking!"

Oh, how easy it is to become tormented by the other-than-the-facts of life. I mean, life would be fine . . .

- ◆ other than the fact that I'm divorced.
- ◆ other than the fact that my father abused me.
- ◆ other than the fact that my family has disowned me.
- ◆ other than the fact that . . . well, just fill in your own blank.

We tend to become so depressed or irate about our circumstances. But what we don't realize is that the other-than-the-facts of life are often the very tools God chooses to use to help get us unstuck from our Small World! That certainly was true in Joseph's life.

GRANTED IMMUNITY

Two years later, Pharaoh had a dream. And when no one in the whole kingdom could interpret his dream, the cupbearer, seeing a chance to score some brownie points, said, "I know somebody who can tell you all about that dream! It's a dude I met in prison named Joseph!"

They brought Joseph before Pharaoh, Joseph interpreted his dream, and Pharaoh was so thrilled—he immediately promoted Joseph to the number two position in Egypt! Wow. One day, he was locked in a dungeon; the next, he was the second most powerful man in the world. Talk about a meteoric promotion!

And because Pharaoh's dream was about a coming famine, Joseph was put in charge of making sure Egypt would have all the food she'd need to survive that famine.

Let's fast-forward to the final episode in this story. Guess who came to tribal council (several years later) looking for food? Yep, Joseph's brothers. The very ones who had created Joseph's *stuckness*. Unbelievably, they were now unknowingly bowing before little brother, just as Joseph's childhood dream predicted they would.

And that's why you should be real careful whenever you angrily scorn the other-than-the-facts of your life. Because if Joseph's brothers had never sold him into slavery, Joseph never would've worked for Potiphar . . . and he never would've been accused of rape . . . and he never would've been put in prison . . . and he never would've met the cupbearer . . . and he never would've interpreted his dream . . . and the cupbearer never would've remembered Joseph when Pharaoh had *his* dream!

But because all these things *did* happen, when the famine hit, Joseph's family had a place where they could come! And Joseph, uniquely placed by God, was able to feed his family and give them a new home.

In what would be his last tribal council, Joseph was large and in charge. Talk about immunity! He sat on a throne, controlled all the food, had all the clout . . . and had in hand *the* perfect opportunity to vote all his brothers right off the planet!

And we'd understand if he had done just that. But instead, when it finally came time to vote something off his island—to get rid of it, to banish it forever from his life—Joseph decided to get rid of . . . his past. All that garbage he'd endured, all the abuse, the injustice, and the neglect. Joseph released every last memory.

It's not that he *denied* the pain his brothers had caused. There was no Pollyanna-ish denial. Joseph had spent several years sifting through all that pain. He even made it clear to them that he knew their intent was, in fact, to hurt him. Genesis 50:20 says, "You intended to harm me, but God intended it for good to accomplish what is now being done, the saving of many lives." He didn't pretend that all was well, that none of this ever bothered him.

He fully acknowledged his pain and the role his brothers played in causing it. But then he . . . let . . . it . . . go.

THE KEY TO WINNING

In your *Survivor* story, you need to do the same thing. You've got to vote your past off *your* island too! So maybe you never got to wear the family coat. Maybe somebody else was the family favorite, never you. Maybe your father didn't love you. Maybe he hurt you, even abused you. Maybe your siblings were a constant source of distress to you. Maybe you never got the family blessing!

He refused to let his brothers' bad behavior dictate *his* behavior.

Here's the problem: as long as you keep clinging to that sad story, rehearsing it and reworking it, remembering it, and rehashing it over and over and over in your mind, you will remain forever imprisoned by *and* paralyzed by your past. Your life will be hindered—spiritually, emotionally, and physically—until you make the willful choice to no longer let your past influence you.

Joseph could've blamed his heartless brothers for . . . you name it: his prison record, his former slave status, plus a whole litany of related issues. But he didn't. He made the hard choice to rise above all those ugly, repressive other-than-the-facts. Instead of just mindlessly continuing his family's genetic predisposition for division, dysfunction, and disharmony, Joseph decided to do what was right.

He didn't get there overnight. Joseph made the extremely difficult decision to move from a position of *emotional reactivity* to a far better place called *mature proactivity*. He refused to let his brothers' bad behavior dictate *his* behavior. He took full responsibility for making the first move.

Interesting word, *responsibility*. If you break it down, its meaning is so clear: "response ability." Put those two words together and . . . voilà! It's the ability to choose your response!

And that's what Joseph exercised. Instead of just reacting impulsively, Joseph chose a more thoughtful response. When he gave his brothers that food, when he invited them to come live with him, he essentially gave absolute immunity to everyone who had hurt him. And when he did, he set himself free most of all. He broke the family chain. And because he did, Joseph was stuck no more.

There is no such thing as a perfect family, which means no one escapes childhood without scars. No matter how godly your parents were or how ideal your home environment, every family is still comprised of imperfect people. And as a result, we've all got scars.

But like Joseph, you have a choice to make. You can stay angry for the rest of your life . . . if you choose. You can continue to carry your wounds into adulthood and live out the balance of your days in constant agitation and irritation. But as long as you keep *reacting* to your past instead of *responding* to your past—you lose.

Walk across the bridge

A better option is to build a bridge and move on! You need to make peace with your past and then vote that past *forever* off your island! Look at the heartache of your life—not from where you sit but from where the God of Heaven resides. The only way you can heal is to cross the bridge of Genesis 50:20—and learn to look at your life through the eyes of Heaven.

If you keep viewing yourself only through the lens of those who've hurt you, it's amazing how powerful you allow those people to become. Their accusations can convince you that maybe you *are* as bad (or stupid or unworthy) as they say you are.

It's only when you look at your life through God's eyes that true healing begins. When you . . .

◆ resist the temptation to keep focusing on the problem and, instead, patiently wait for God to provide his solution.

◆ refuse to focus on yourself and get all wrapped up in self-pity. Instead, choose to believe that God is in control; he's directing this play that you're starring in.

◆ release the need to blame somebody—constantly nursing your wounds and cursing your accusers.

Actually, God has already built the bridge. All you have to do is walk across it by mustering enough faith to refuse to accept your life as everybody has defined it for you. You refuse to give up, and you never give in.

Stop turning moments into monuments—that's what keeps you wallowing in this mess.

In faith, you take a baby step across that bridge. And then another and another . . . until you begin to sense a ferocious determination rising within you—so that if another step is what you need to take to complete your trek to the other side, you'll take it, even if it's the very step everybody else in your life says is impossible.

That's what Joseph did.

Keep moving forward

Then once you get to the other side, don't dare look back. Don't light a candle and hold some private vigil. And don't build a monument to past pain. Let your past be just a moment. Stop turning moments into monuments—that's what keeps you wallowing in this mess.

Instead, once you cross the bridge, keep moving. And if you have to, repeat this truth to yourself: I cannot alter my history, but I can change the way my history is altering me.

Cross that bridge God has built for you. And keep moving. Like Joseph did.

Sometime between Joseph's elevation to prime minister and the first time he was reunited with his brothers, Joseph got married and fathered two sons. Any clue as to what he named his boys? Back then, parents didn't choose their kiddos' names just because they sounded nice. "Bocephus—that's it . . . or . . . how about Ricky Bobby?"

Because Joseph had chosen to view his life through Heaven's eyes, God was invited to remove every sting from every memory.

No, they gave their children names of significance. Genesis 41:51 says, "Joseph named his firstborn Manasseh . . . 'because [*he said, and get this*] God has made me forget all my trouble.'"

The verse essentially reads, "God has 'Manassehed' me all my trouble." The root of *Manasseh* is *nashah*, and it means "to forget."[2] In the term's full construct, *Manasseh* suggests that the bitter sting out of all those painful memories had finally and forever been removed.

Joseph had many painful memories from his past. But because Joseph had chosen to view his life through Heaven's eyes, God was invited to remove every sting from every memory. And Joseph celebrated his healing by naming his firstborn Manasseh: God made me forget.

When offspring number two came along, Joseph named him Ephraim "because God has made me fruitful in the land of my suffering" (v. 52). Joseph was acknowledging, "God 'Ephraimed' me. He made me . . . fruitful."

Joseph named both boys God Made Me: God Made Me Forget . . . and God Made Me Fruitful! In other words, "God was always with me, and because he refused to give up on me, I didn't just survive my family unit—God has made me to thrive!"

Joseph didn't *really* forget what had been done to him. That's impossible! But because he kept his eyes on God and because he trusted in God's perfect plan, he found that bitterness had no place to grow. And his cynicism—and yes, those painful wounds—also healed and faded away. How did it happen? Because God can touch us in places no therapist could ever reach.

Every time Joseph saw little Manasseh, he remembered how God had helped him forget. And Ephraim too. Instead of being angry for all that abuse, Joseph realized something you may still need to learn: that God had used his deepest heartache for a greater good, a nobler purpose . . . a higher goal. That's what God does. He makes us fruitful in the very place of our deepest heartache. Life breaks down for everybody sometime. But thank God, through his power we can grow strong even in the broken places—or maybe *because* of them.

Maybe you're not there yet. May I urge you to make a firm resolve in your heart to get there? To make a firm decision even now that you will no longer allow your past to hold you captive. Instead of cursing what happened to you, why not give birth to a Manasseh instead? Maybe not a flesh and blood baby. But build something—or buy something—and name it Manasseh!

That's what I did. While in the blackest hole of my deepest pain, I found a small eagle. (I collect eagles.) When I got this eagle, I'd just received some ugly news that shook my whole world. But still wanting to trust God, I named my new eagle Manasseh. And to this day, whenever I see that eagle, I claim the truth of this story—for me. And I thank God for taking the sting away, for healing me in all my broken places.

Does my past still hurt? Of course it does. But the sting is gone forever.

What God did for Joseph, and what God has done for me, he wants to do for you too. But he can't—not without your permission.

There's one last tribal council. You are surrounded by the other members of your tribe—whoever is a support and a help to you. Torches are aflame, the muffled sound of a crashing surf provides a musical backdrop. Your name is called. It's your turn. It's time for you to cross the bridge and, in absolute privacy, mark your ballot. So you take the pen in hand, and you're kind of nervous because you're just about to vote something very significant out of your life forever.

You write just two words on that parchment, two words that represent a far greater control on your heart and happiness than your abuser could ever exert over you. Two words that have haunted you more than anything else: M-Y P-A-S-T.

Whatever your past is, whatever those words represent for you, write them down. As you write, vote all that ugly, depressing, faith-stealing, hope-robbing, love-harming *past* garbage off your island . . . and out of your life forever!

And if you can't find the strength to do it alone, call a friend. And call on Jesus. When you do, Jesus will step into the remaining void. He will "Manasseh" your past for you.

You ask him. And I promise he will come through . . . after all.

WHERE
TO
BEGIN

Genesis 45:16—46:30

➡ PEOPLE LIKE YOU

Peter was the outcast growing up in his family. He was not the athlete, he was not the favored, and he was not the one who did things that the family bragged about.

Over time, he developed a rather large disdain for his family, especially his father and brother. He lived his life out of anger and resentment, which contributed to his path of multiple addictions. His life was so full of past and festering pain that the first thing he reached for in the morning—even before getting out of bed so he wouldn't have to feel a minute of pain—was his favorite addiction waiting on the nightstand.

Throughout his first wife's alcoholism and then terminal illness, he continued his addictive lifestyle. When he decided to turn his life around, he was alone.

He returned home to his father and brother to address his issues with them, but found them unreceptive. He forged ahead anyway, knowing what was best for him. He took responsibility for the mistakes of his own life and sought help by being accountable to friends.

When his father began addressing his own baggage, their relationship turned; and they became the best of friends. The trust took time to rebuild and was not without its share of trial and error, lots of pain and tears. Forgiveness was a work in progress. Listening was a key factor . . . on both sides. Sometimes it takes a son to heal a father.

My son Josh was going through some difficult stuff, and I was his sounding board. It's a conversation this dad will treasure for a lifetime. As I listened to his pain, I started flashing back to when I was a high school freshman. And as his experiences triggered memories of my past, I realized something: for the average male, there is no more awkward and downright repressive time—perhaps in all of life—than when he's a freshman in high school.

- You're too old to ride your bike, but too young to drive a car.
- You're surrounded by beautiful, young women—none of whom has any desire to date a freshman.
- Your voice jumps two octaves even when you don't want it to.
- Zits pop up in the most unusual places and at the most inopportune times.
- Your body is growing faster than your ability to control it—and your feet trip over everything from rubber bands to full-length sofas!

Josh was struggling with some of those things as well as relationship issues. He was also disappointed by some choices his peers were making . . . and was trying to piece through some of the debris of our own family turmoil.

I said, "Hang in there, OK? It won't be like this forever. This is a tough year, no doubt. But hold on. Life *will* come to you. Till then, keep your head up and your heart right—and someday everything you want *and* need will come to you. I promise."

We hugged and he headed for bed. But as I switched off my light and reached for my pillow, I realized that the same message my son needed to hear was what his dad needed to hear even more: "Be patient. Life will come to you. Just hang in there, OK?"

As I lay all alone in my way-too-wide bed, mindlessly

staring at the ceiling fan slowly spinning in the shadows, I wondered, *Do I really believe that? I mean, I've been waiting a long time for life to come back to me—do I still believe that it will?*

Joseph's time *did* come. It took a while, but it finally happened. Even more, his fractured family was restored! A rare feat in Bible accounts, I'm afraid. And unless I miss my guess, equally rare in your family.

Between the lines of Joseph's story, we watch God doing what God loves to do: healing broken hearts, restoring fractured lives, transforming desperate circumstances, and reconciling shattered families.

You remember the devastation. Joseph's dad had four wives, twelve sons, and one daughter—but he loved Joseph most of all. Talk about a discombobulated family! Daddy playin' favorites. Four "mommies" spending all their time primping, hoping, *Maybe Jake the Beefcake will pick* me *tonight.*

I lay all alone in my way-too-wide bed, mindlessly staring at the ceiling fan slowly spinning in the shadows.

It was in that leadership vacuum that Joseph's ten older brothers, who despised Joseph, concocted a plan to sell him to traders headed for Egypt. Eventually, Joseph landed in prison with an extended sentence. And the only reason he even got out of prison was because Pharaoh had a dream . . . and Joseph, through God's power, could interpret dreams. The dream concerned a coming famine. And Pharaoh, utterly impressed with Joseph, decided that Joseph was the only one capable enough to lead Operation Famine Prep. The famine arrived, and at some point during that seven-year plague, Joseph's dad sent Joseph's brothers to Egypt—the only place on the planet where hungry people could find food.

THE REST OF THE STORY

Joseph's brothers had no clue that the lord of the land before whom they stood—and who held in his hands their destiny—was the little brother they had tossed into that pit two long decades ago. Joseph must have dreamed of this moment, conjuring up images of his brothers groveling, pleading for mercy just as they'd made him plead. And in the dream, payback time was soooo sweet: *Finally! My chance to get even with those dirtbags! My brothers will rue the day they ditched me in that pit. I've endured slavery and jail. I've known heartache and desperation as no man should ever have to know! But now my time has come!*

And at first, that's exactly how Joseph intended to play this hand. He clearly understood that his brothers had intended to harm him (see Genesis 50:20). Perhaps he had attempted to suppress twenty years of rage, which boiled violently within him until that day, when standing before him were those very brothers.

The human spirit is not made for revenge.

The account in Genesis 42 indicates some ways in which Joseph put his brothers through the wringer:

◆ He accused them of being spies.

◆ He threatened to keep one of them as his slave.

◆ He put their silver back in their grain sacks, a move that "frightened" (v. 35) them to no end. They figured he'd accuse them of stealing again, which would effectively cut off any future food trips. In that case, if the famine continued, their whole family would die.

Did Joseph's little payback game work? Did Joseph punk 'em? Abso-stinkin'-lutely!

"They said to one another, 'Surely we are being punished

because of our brother. We saw how distressed he was when he pleaded with us for his life, but we would not listen; that's why this distress has come upon us'" (v. 21).

Brother Reuben added, "We must give an accounting for [Joseph's] blood" (v. 22). So obviously these brothers—who had already endured twenty years of private guilt—were finally openly acknowledging their guilt.

On the downside, this encounter had been so distressing, the brothers never wanted to see Egypt again. Even when their food supply was once again tapped out, dad practically had to order them to return (see Genesis 43:1-14). Joseph's time had finally come! But because he was more into affixing blame than healing scars, his blame led to his brothers' shame; but it didn't heal even one morsel of his family's pain.

Then something strange happened, and I think it happened as Joseph watched his brothers trudge back toward Canaan. Joseph evidently realized, *I didn't enjoy that nearly as much as I thought I would. It felt good in my dreams, but getting even wasn't all that satisfying!*

He didn't like the person he had become. He who hated his brothers for being so cruel that they would laugh as he begged for mercy was now doing exactly the same thing to them. He had discovered that the human spirit is not made for revenge. Paybacks, tirades, blame-placing, and finger-pointing take a greater toll on the one aiming the finger than they do on the one at whom that finger points.

Between the time his brothers left and the time they would return, Joseph had an awakening. He finally arrived at acceptance. He finally decided, *The only way I'm gonna heal is if I stop acting like a victim and assume full responsibility for my own recovery.*

In Genesis 43 the brothers returned for more food. Once again, they stood before the lord of Egypt. He was actually their brother, but he looked like an Egyptian, talked like an Egyptian, and (*ahem*) walked like an Egyptian. (Sorry.)

They didn't know it was him, but *he* knew it was *them*. Even though he had already forgiven them, Joseph still gave them one last pop quiz, this time honestly hoping that they would pass his test with flying colors.

We need to be quick to forgive but slow to trust.

I believe Joseph *forgave* his brothers sometime between these two road trips, but he still wasn't sure if it was safe enough to *trust* his brothers. Some Christians teach that forgiveness is accomplished only if everybody kisses, makes up, and pretends that nothing ever happened. But that's like spraying perfume on a pig and pretending he doesn't stink!

True forgiveness releases my right, and even my desire, to hurt you for hurting me. Never mind what you did to me—I'm laying down my arms and burying the hatchet. If our broken relationship has any chance of being renewed, in addition to forgiveness there also has to be *trust*. But unlike forgiveness, trust isn't a gift; it must be earned.

Joseph's story teaches us something we don't hear nearly enough: we need to be quick to forgive but slow to trust. I know, that sounds *so* wrong. But John 2:24 says, "Jesus didn't trust [certain people], because he knew what people were really like" (*NLT*).

Forgiveness should be swift because we don't want to become angry, bitter, hard-hearted, and mean-spirited people. But trusting takes time. If your spouse cheated on you, then returned saying, "I'm sorry," of course you should forgive. But it's OK to add, "Before we go any further though, I need to see the change." Trust can be lost in an instant, but it's re-earned ever so slowly.

A TEST OF TRUST

Joseph wasn't being a jerk. He was just trying to figure out, *Where are my brothers coming from?* He devised a test comprised of three very probing questions.

The first question

The first question came when Joseph served a lavish meal with his brothers as his guests of honor. However, his little brother, Benjamin—his only full-blood brother—was given (per Joseph's instruction) "five times as much as ... the others" (Genesis 43:34, *NLT*).

Joseph wanted to know, *Did any of those old jealousies get transferred to Dad's second favorite son? I mean, will they be jealous and start growling if Benjy gets more? Or will they just enjoy their own full plates and rejoice in Benjy's four bonus plates?*

Throughout the whole meal, Joseph kept one trained eye on body language. He studied his brothers' faces, he watched their nonverbal exchanges, he strained to find even one hint that this random act of kindness was cleaning their clocks. But there was no such hint. Instead, "they feasted and drank freely with him" (v. 34).

After dinner, it was time for the brothers to head home. As they were leaving, "Joseph gave these instructions to the steward of his house: 'Fill the men's sacks with as much food as they can carry, and put each man's silver in the mouth of his sack. Then put my cup, the silver one, in the mouth of the youngest one's sack. . . .' And he did as Joseph said" (44:1, 2). Long before Cracker Jack, Joseph slipped a prize in Benjy's sack.

The second question

Soon after their departure, Joseph dispatched his steward to find them and ask, "Why have you repaid an act of kindness with such evil? What do you mean by stealing my master's personal silver drinking cup, which he uses to predict the future? What a wicked thing you have done!" (vv. 4, 5, *NLT*).

Joseph didn't need goblets and sorcery to see into the future. His power came from God. And this silver goblet was merely a prop to protect Joseph's Egyptian cover. Still, the brothers vigorously protested their innocence and made an offer: "If you find his cup with any one of us, let that one die. And all the rest of us will be your master's slaves forever" (v. 9, *NLT*).

"Each of them quickly lowered his sack to the ground and opened it. . . . And the cup was found [*uh-oh*] in Benjamin's sack" (vv. 11, 12).

Here was the chance to explore question number two on Joseph's mind: *Given the chance, would my brothers dispose of Benjy? They gave* me *away . . . would they throw Ben under the bus too?*

Here's the answer: "At this, [the brothers] tore their clothes. Then they all loaded their donkeys and returned to the city" (v. 13). Can you imagine Joseph's relief as he watched that familiar caravan wind its way back into the city? Not just Benjamin, but the entire band of brothers?

"When Judah and his brothers came in, . . . they threw themselves to the ground before him. Joseph said to them, 'What is this you have done? Don't you know that a man like me can find things out by divination?'

"'What can we say to my lord?' Judah replied. . . . 'How can we prove our innocence? God has uncovered your servants' guilt. We are now my lord's slaves—we ourselves and the one who was found to have the cup'" (vv. 14-16).

Let's reset that scene. Benjamin was in chains. The others were huddled around Judah, their spokesman, and he stepped forward to plead their case.

I can picture Judah years earlier, dipping Joseph's coat in goat's blood, then consoling dad at Joseph's funeral (even though he knew the truth). Judah also married a woman as evil as he was, and they had two sons so despicable that God actually struck them dead! (see 38:1-10).

Judah was one bad boy—a bad brother, a bad husband, a bad father, and a bad son. But not anymore. We don't know when, but at some point Judah changed. And Judah is just one example that change really *can* happen! He was a scoundrel, now a saint. Judah didn't just accept himself as a bad man and make excuses for his behavior. No, he was different. And now he was talking to this Egyptian (without a clue that it was really his brother).

When Judah offered his whole band of brothers as slaves, "Joseph said, 'Far be it from me to do such a thing! Only the man who was found to have the cup will become my slave. The rest of you, go back to your father in peace'" (v. 17). See his plan? Joseph put Benjamin in the very place he had been two decades before. "You guys can go, but I'm keeping Ben."

Then he waited. *Will my brothers go to bat for Benjy? They didn't go to bat for me! But if they* do *step up, then I'll know they really have changed.*

In Genesis 44:18-34 Judah, so evil before yet now so committed to righteousness, made one of the most impassioned pleas for mercy you'll find anywhere. Judah no longer thought only about himself; he was now worried about dad. Judah told Joseph about his other brother from a different mother, the one dad believed (but Judah knew better) had been "torn to pieces" (v. 28).

I'm convinced Joseph's heart leaped within him when he heard those words. For twenty years he might have wondered, *How come Dad hasn't come looking for me? I thought he loved me. We seemed close—what with the coat and all—but maybe he doesn't care about me . . . after all!* Well,

Joseph finally got his answer: dad never came because Joseph's brothers lied. They had reported him dead.

Maybe you've wondered the same thing. Your dad walked out on you; he's not there for you. And there's this ache in your heart that wonders, *Why won't Dad come looking for me?*

Sometimes we have no clue what others have gone through to get where they are today. You may have no idea the heartache your mom or dad experienced when they were kids. You just don't know. Don't put everything your family does to you under the microscope of your own limited perspective.

I remember the day my parents told me their stories. I wept for them—and for me. I learned that there's always more to the story, and I also learned to unconditionally love my parents and give them a lot more slack than before.

Judah said, "So my lord, if Dad sees us coming home and Benjy isn't there, he will die" (see v. 31). Then he volunteered to take the place of Benjamin so that Benjamin could return to his father. He couldn't bear to go home and tell dad his *other* favorite son was also dead.

Twenty years before, Judah had no such emotions. As Joseph begged for mercy, vainly trying to scramble from that pit, Judah walked away. But now, instead of "Let's kill him," Judah offered, "Let me die for him. I wanna be his substitute."

You may have no idea the heartache your mom or dad experienced when they were kids.

By the way, of Israel's twelve tribes (each descended from one of these brothers), Jesus came out of the tribe of Judah (Revelation 5:5; Matthew 1:2; Hebrews 7:14). Wow. In this, Judah's moment of personal triumph, he also set into motion his family's new Small World story, a story that would climax on a hill outside Jerusalem when we were "made holy through the sacrifice of the body of Jesus Christ once for all" (Hebrews 10:10).

Now finally! The part of the story we've all been waiting for . . .

"Joseph could no longer control himself before all his attendants, and he cried out, 'Have everyone leave my presence!' So there was no one with Joseph when he made himself known to his brothers" (Genesis 45:1).

This was partly because Joseph was about to lose it, and men don't usually cry in front of other men. It was also because Joseph knew this was family business and it needed to remain family business. Follow Joseph's lead, and keep family stuff in the family.

Imagine your rebellious child just showing up at your door after years of rebellion, and she says, "I'm sorry. Can I come home?"

Maybe it's a phone call: "This is your father. I know you don't trust me, but if you could ever find it in your heart to forgive me, I'll never let you down again."

Perhaps it's an e-mail from a once-dear friend who writes, "You'll never know how sorry I am for the role I played in your heartache."

Ever had an experience like that?

◆ Your mom abandoned you.
◆ Your dad drank away your childhood.
◆ Your spouse ran off with someone else.

But now he or she is back and would really like to work things out. What do you do in a moment like that? That's *this* moment for Joseph. He cleared the room, took a loud and much-deserved cry, and then he (not his interpreter) said— in Hebrew, their own native tongue—"I am Joseph!" (v. 3).

And verily, verily, his brethren answered and saith unto

him, "Where's your bathroom?" Nah, it doesn't say that, but trust me ... that's what happened!

The third question

After Joseph identified himself, the next item on his agenda was not to ask, "What kind of jerks would do what you did to me?"

That's what *I* would ask.

But Joseph asked, "How's Dad? Is Dad still alive?" (see v. 3).

"But his brothers were not able to answer him, because they were terrified" (v. 3).

"Then Joseph said . . . , 'Come close to me'" (v. 4). That means more than you think it means. After all, they were already alone. Why come closer? I think it's because Joseph wanted to open his robe and reveal his circumcision. Surely that would prove his identity! Back then, circumcision was *the* proof of Hebrew authenticity. So when they came close, they saw—and Joseph said, "I am your brother Joseph, the one you sold into Egypt!" (v. 4).

If that had been you and me, we'd really punch that last phrase and launch into a tirade to end all tirades! But not Joseph. Not this time. Instead he said, "Do not be distressed and do not be angry with yourselves for selling me here" (v. 5).

Say what?

BURY IT

Sometimes we dream of moments when that certain someone will finally get around to apologizing, because we can't wait to unload both barrels! Joseph had plenty of shell casings in his bag too.

- ◆ "You guys separated me from my dad."
- ◆ "My sons have never met their granddad."

- "We were brothers, but you don't even know who I am!"
- "I spent my teen years as a slave and my twenties locked in prison. I've got a record, thanks to you!"

And there was a time, not that long ago, when Joseph gladly would've gone there! Maybe you can understand. But do you know what that loaded shotgun you carry around is saying about you? It's saying you haven't forgiven. It's saying your heart is bitter and your passion is all about revenge.

Years ago, a man I thought was a friend stormed into my office with a stack of napkins and old envelopes in hand. And on those papers were scrawled eighteen years of rage! My "friend" had chronicled on random slips of paper, over a period of almost two decades, every disappointment and every failure he had chosen to assign to me! And evidently this was the day when all those bills had come due.

As I sat there listening to his harangue, at first I felt angry. But then my anger turned to sorrow for him (to have to live inside such a miserable shell)—and even more, for his family. If the man had that many notes on *me,* how many more must he have on *them*!

When someone (about whom you've felt that you would lose it if he ever apologized) finally *does* apologize, forgive him. By all means test him before you fully trust him. But immediately forgive him. In fact, go ahead and forgive him even before he apologizes. Empty the chambers in your shotgun and release the anger in your heart so that when you finally *do* receive that knock at the door, instead of giving that person a refresher on exactly how badly you were done wrong . . . you'll be able to forgive.

Maybe you *can* blame certain family members for everything bad about your life, but don't do it. Bury the offense, and keep it buried.

A preacher's son wanted to be just like his daddy. So when his cat died, he decided this was the perfect opportunity to do his first funeral, just like daddy. He grabbed a shoe box, carved a hole in the end, put the body of the cat inside, stuck the tail through the hole he'd carved, then put the lid on and secured it with two rubber bands. With his parents watching, he dug a shallow grave, held a brief service, and then buried the cat. All but the tail, that is. He left the tail sticking out of the ground.

He explained, "I'm gonna have another funeral tomorrow. So I'll just yank the tail and out comes my cat!"

His parents reluctantly agreed to his plan, so for several days he did it—till one day he pulled the tail . . . and the tail came off! That's when they decided it was time to bury everything.

But that's what *we* do, isn't it? We forgive, but we like keeping the tail out just in case we wanna dig it *all* up all over again. Or in the likely event the person slips up once more, we can let him have it.

Just bury the cat! That's what Joseph did.

But God . . .

Joseph forgave his brothers even before he had confronted them. His forgiveness had already been granted because he cultivated the right perspective. In verse 5 Joseph said, "It was to save lives that God sent me ahead of you." This is a diagnosis that took Joseph twenty years to figure out, but this verse is exactly why Joseph was able to forgive. He finally realized that his *brothers* didn't sell him into Egypt— *God* did. ("Boys, we didn't realize it at the time, but God arranged all the pieces in our family puzzle. Having looked into the future and having seen a famine on its way, God sent me here!")

Joseph said, "For two years now there has been famine in the land, and for the next five years there will not be plowing and reaping. But God sent me ahead of you to preserve for you a remnant on earth and to save your lives by a great deliverance" (vv. 6, 7).

In other words, "Yeah, your motives were lousy, but God . . . No, you never should've hurt me like that, but God . . . There were times in prison when I just wanted to fling myself beneath the threshing stone and be done with this cold, hard world, but God . . ."

But God . . .

That's the key to starting over again. It's the very place where your healing has got to begin. God did not create all the pain you've had to go through, but he will use it to accomplish his will in your life.

Joseph forgave his brothers even before he had confronted them.

The curtain closed with Joseph inviting his whole family to ride out the famine with him in Egypt. And then, in an especially touching scene, Joseph "kissed all his brothers and wept over them" (v. 15).

Sadly, that kind of healing doesn't happen very often. As far as we know, it didn't happen for Isaac and Ishmael—even though they did come together to bury their father (25:9). We hope Jacob and Esau's recorded reunion (chap. 33) represented a permanent fix. Bad family chains can be broken! Joseph's family, as dysfunctional and messed up as it obviously was, found a way to come together again.

And that's why it's always too early to jump ship. This Small World family spent three generations in the dumpster. But God . . .

Where do you begin so you can start again? Wait for God's perfect moment of restoration and healing. Wait for life to come to you again. And as you wait, keep your head up and your heart right.

But God . . .

Those two words are the only way you can get started again
. . . after all.

DELIVERING A DELIVERER

Exodus 1:8-22; 2:1-10

➡️ PEOPLE LIKE YOU

The power of a praying mother cannot be underestimated. The results are often not realized for a long time, and sometimes *never* known.

There are countless stories of parents who prayed as they waded through the trials and tribulations of a child's adolescent years, only to wait twenty more years to see where their child ended up. Becky was a mother who knelt beside the rocking chair where she had years earlier rocked her son, now pleading with God to change his heart. And Ellen quietly prayed over her sleeping daughter every night as they struggled for a relationship they both could tolerate.

Numerous other stories of prayer began much earlier, whether the young child was dealing with a disability or there was some other extenuating circumstance that affected the family system. Take Rachel, for example. Each morning the first thing she did was ask God to comfort and guide her children, because she knew she and her husband were inadequate in doing so.

There is strong research that lends credibility to the power of prayer in people's lives—whether they are sick or dealing with stress or with unknown circumstances.

Who are your heroes? Who functions as your North Star? Who has already climbed the mountain yet stands tall on its conquered peak, beckoning you to continue your climb too?

Heroes not only reflect the kind of person we can become, they actually *urge* us to become. They inspire us by proving the capacity we possess for greatness. They are authentic men and women who have flaws and have experienced failure just like us, except they don't try to hide it.

They are stouthearted people who aren't afraid to be different and who are willing, even eager, to take risks. They were not necessarily blessed with the greatest skill, but they maximized every ounce of the skill they did possess.

GIVE ME THE BACK STORY

When I was a kid, I looked up to heroes. As a teen, I wanted to be like my heroes. And now as a road-worn baby boomer, with more time behind me than I have before me, I find myself looking beyond the external heroics. Instead of just admiring my heroes and trying to imitate them, I want to know, "How did they get where they are?"

I want to know the story *behind* the story. How is it that they stood strong and kept their edge even in the face of incredible, seemingly insurmountable odds? And how is it that even though they fell, they got up . . . and started climbing again?

One of my more recent heroes is Lance Armstrong. I'm not saying that every aspect of his life is heroic and worthy of imitation. I'm just saying, put a bicycle under his legs and something transcendent happens.

In his book *It's Not About the Bike,* Lance tells his story: how a world-class athlete who got testicular cancer at age twenty-five nearly died. Yet four years later, he won the Tour de France, the 2,300-mile road race considered to be the most grueling sporting event on earth. Add six more consecutive wins to his résumé, and you have a record that may never be equaled.

But it's not Lance's winning streak that compelled me to add him to my list of heroes. It wasn't his lyrical climb through the Alps nor his heroic conquering of the Pyrenees. What grabbed my heart is that this world-class athlete who'd worked so hard—exercising personal discipline and self-denial in his drive to be the world's greatest biker—was suddenly sidelined. Because of the nature of his disease, he couldn't even sit on a bike, let alone ride one.

Through sheer determination and guts, and after a long, arduous bout with discouragement and thoughts of just giving up, Lance climbed back on his bike again. And he not only rode once more, he conquered the most vicious obstacle of all—his own fear. That's when he decided to race again. And when he did . . . it's almost a sidebar, but he won.

He won!

Lance writes: "I'm asking you now, at the outset, to put aside your ideas about heroes and miracles, because I'm not storybook material. This is not Disneyland, or Hollywood. I'll give you an example: I've read that I *flew* up the hills and mountains of France. But you don't fly up a hill. You struggle slowly and painfully up a hill, and maybe, if you work very hard, you get to the top ahead of everybody else."[1]

Maybe.

Then again, who cares, as long as you get there? It's not the win that makes Lance a hero; it's his struggle. It's not that he climbed those mountains faster than everybody else climbed them; it's that he decided the climb was worth it. Then having decided to climb in the face of unimaginable resistance, he kept pedaling anyway.

How do you keep pedaling when you've decided to climb but you're not sure you can make it? when you're stuck between your dream and your dread? What do you do?

FROM BIKES TO BULRUSHES

Around 1500 BC, life was pretty sweet for the Hebrews. Years before, there'd been a famine in the land, yet one of their own not only saved them but all of Egypt as well! If it hadn't been for Joseph, Egypt would have starved. And the king of Egypt, known as Pharaoh, was so grateful to Joseph that he invited Joseph's whole family to come live with him in a choice new development called Goshen.

As a result, the Hebrews enjoyed high-ranking political connections in the most powerful nation on earth, plus they lived in the most fertile piece of land in the land! Which is why, for years the Israelites just kinda hung out and made babies! Lots of babies! The Bible says, "Their descendants had many children and grandchildren. In fact, they multiplied so quickly that they soon filled the land" (Exodus 1:7, *NLT*).

Even more, they also rested in God's promise that one day he would deliver them from Egypt and take them to a promised land—their own land—a land overflowing with milk and honey.

Picture row after row of shabby little shanties filled with way too many kids and not nearly enough food.

But "a new king came to the throne of Egypt who knew nothing about Joseph or what he had done" (v. 8, *NLT*). Evidently this *new* king hadn't boned up on Egyptian history and had no clue about Joseph's heroic save. Somehow it escaped him that were it not for Joseph's Operation Famine Prep, Egypt would have been reduced to dust.

The new Pharaoh took one look at this exceedingly fertile bunch of immigrants . . . and got scared! He was afraid Israel might join forces with his enemies to attack Egypt. He was also afraid Israel might even leave (vv. 9, 10). Talk about stuck! Pharaoh couldn't live *with* them, but he didn't want to live *without* them!

PHARAOH'S POWER PLAY

Pharaoh launched a vicious threefold attack he hoped would put the hurtin' on that Hebrew baby-makin' factory.

Plan A: demoralize

"Forced labor" (v. 11) is the term Scripture uses, as these descendants of former honored guests now labored in the hot Egyptian sun, building ego palaces for Egyptian royals. Instead of making babies they were hauling mud, digging sand, drawing water—building bricks. Then they took those bricks and built storehouses in which the pharaohs could stack mountains of provisions and possibly even armor and other battle gear, as well as treasures.

Pharaoh believed such labor would cripple the Hebrews. But the Bible says, "The more they were oppressed, the more they multiplied" (v. 12). That doesn't mean they didn't suffer. No, they did the backbreaking work Egyptians refused to do—and for far less pay.

As time passed, Goshen became a ghetto. Picture row after row of shabby little shanties filled with way too many kids and not nearly enough food. Plus two overworked, totally exhausted parents who had little time for the kiddos and *no* time for each other.

Add to their suffering the blatant sensuality of that pagan land—where Egypt's national religion included sexual deviations of every type. Some people believe the Hebrews would have been used as trinkets in Egyptian worship: Hebrew women, for example, raped and then left for dead, Hebrew children sodomized and then discarded. It was a dark and despicably evil time, yet the Israelites proved remarkably resilient.

Pharaoh moved to plan B

Pharaoh proclaimed a royal mandate that every Hebrew midwife was to "accidentally" suffocate every male Hebrew newborn.

He said, "When you help the Hebrew women in childbirth and observe them on the delivery stool ..." (v. 16). That term *delivery stool* means "two stones." The midwife brought two hollowed-out rocks; the mother-to-be sat on those rocks and dropped the baby into the waiting arms of her midwife. (Sound exciting, ladies?) When that happens, Pharaoh said, "if it is a boy, kill him" (v. 16).

Thankfully, the midwives loved God more than they feared Pharaoh, and they "did not do what the king of Egypt had told them to do" (v. 17).

Enter Pharaoh's plan C

He pronounced another royal decree for the entire Hebrew population: every newborn male "you must throw into the Nile" (v. 22).

The Israelites would live in bondage for 430 years! That's a long time to wait for deliverance, by anyone's measure. I get antsy waiting for a muffin to warm in the microwave! Tapping my fingers . . . counting down from twenty seconds . . . If I have to stand in line at Target more than three minutes . . . if the light changes, and it's more than 1.7 seconds before the car in front of me hits the gas . . . whenever I have to stand at the fax machine and make sure it sent OK, I'm practically ballistic. I can't even conceive of waiting 430 years!

When you have cancer and life is draining away, you get so tired of waiting; yet you still plead for a miracle. When your child is autistic—and every day is filled with frightening challenges and discouraging setbacks—you wonder, *Will God ever deliver me?* When you've lost your reputation, when you're single but desire to be married, when you've been abused and old wounds absolutely refuse to heal . . . what do you do?

When all you can seem to do is build bricks and stack stones, how do you keep waiting—and *trusting* that God will keep his promise?

WHAT TO DO WHILE STACKING STONES

Exodus 2:23 says, "During that long period, the king of Egypt died." Note that. Even God realized what a long wait this had been. The Israelites "groaned in their slavery."

Denial isn't even an option when you're slogging through mud . . . and building bricks. When your family is constantly exposed to all sorts of sensual idolatry and moral depravity, you can't just pretend that stuff isn't happening. So you groan. The typical, human response to unending suffering and inexplicable pain is to grumble! To carp and complain, to sigh and to whine! That's what the Israelites did.

In fact, they said some of the same stuff we say, like, "I don't deserve this." The only reason they were even in Egypt was because Joseph had saved Egypt. "And this is the thanks we get?" And then there's the ever popular "Why me? Why this? Why now?" diatribe.

When your family is constantly exposed to all sorts of sensual idolatry and moral depravity, you can't just pretend that stuff isn't happening.

When Rick Pitino was coaching the Providence College men's basketball team, his team was awaiting a bid to the NCAA tournament, the Big Dance, when Pitino's son

Daniel, born six months before with congenital heart problems, finally succumbed to his illness. In Pitino's book *Success Is a Choice,* he offers insight into how he endured that incredible loss. He writes:

> Illness, tragedy, and death take us through the entire spectrum of human emotion. They not only make us let go of our dreams but also make us want to give up everything else as well.
>
> How do we overcome personal tragedy and go on?
>
> In the midst of life's most difficult times, the only way to carry on is by being mentally tough. What is that toughness about?
>
> It's the awareness that everything doesn't always have a solution. Some of life's mysteries are just that, mysteries. There are certain things that simply are unknown to us. Call it fate. Call it a belief in a higher being. Give it any definition you want. But these circumstances eventually touch all of us, and we must be tough enough mentally to withstand them. If you think about it, we really have little choice. We either learn how to overcome life's tragedies or we sink into the blackness of despair.[2]

Then he writes: "When it comes to dealing with a personal tragedy, you have a choice. You can either succumb to it and have it drag you down, or you can fight through it and have it make you stronger. It can either cripple you and thwart your dreams or make you realize how precious life is. . . . You have a choice when it comes to dealing with life. You must remain rock-solid positive. Not because it's necessarily the right way. Because it's the only way."[3]

GROWING PAST THE GROANING

Groaning is a very normal and expected human response in the face of suffering! Just don't stay there. Don't simply wave a white flag and surrender. Instead, develop your moral strength and hone your mental toughness to such a degree that if you need to groan, groan already! But don't *stop* with the groaning.

And if you want to cry, cry! But don't just cry into your pillow. If you're gonna cry, at least cry out to the Lord! That's what the Hebrews did: "And their cry for help because of their slavery went up to God" (v. 23).

Growing through your groaning and crying *is* a process. The first sound that comes when misery finds its voice is the groan. The problem is, if you keep groaning even your dog will eventually get tired of hearing it!

At some point, mental toughness has to kick in. And you have a choice to make: *Am I going to just grumble in my special pouting place—and become bitter and sour in the process? Or am I going to make the mentally tough decision to turn my groanings into a heartfelt cry to God?*

PUTTING LORD BEFORE YOUR GROAN

It's a matter of putting *Lord* in front of your distress. What I mean by that is, instead of saying, "This isn't fair!" say instead, "Lord, this doesn't seem fair. What's going on?"

Instead of saying, "I'm sick and tired of all this abuse, and I'm not gonna take it anymore!" say, "Lord, I'm really ticked off—I need answers."

That's how you move from just groaning to actually releasing your heartache to God! Put *Lord* in front of whatever is bugging you!

"Lord, Goshen was once filled with twenty-four-hour buffets, huge piles of money lying around, and nonstop baby-making sessions! But now . . . we're building bricks—

bricks that help the enemy! Lord, we're dying here! You gotta do something!"

Perhaps you're thinking, *I've tried that prayer drill. And it didn't work. I've asked for plenty of stuff, but I never got an answer.*

Time out. Did you really not get an answer or just not get the answer you wanted? God *always* answers. Sometimes he says yes, sometimes he says no, and sometimes—actually lots of times—he says, "Not yet."

What do we do? We start groaning all over again. We want God to break through the clouds—*now*! We want him to do some amazing miracle—today! But when it doesn't work that way, we question whether God actually cares or is even there.

It would be quite some time before God would answer the Israelites' cry. Yet in that sluggish in-between time, they kept taking their heartache to God . . . anyway.

STACKING BRICKS WITH ENTHUSIASM

Not only did they cry out to God, the Israelites refused to die in a pile. Even though all they had to look forward to each day was stacking stones, they kept stacking 'em anyway! Mixing the mortar, shaping the brick . . . laying it in place. Day in and day out . . . year after year . . . for what would end up being four hundred years!

We want God to break through the clouds—*now*! We want him to do some amazing miracle—today!

I know a little something about not being where you thought you'd be. And even more about not doing what you thought you were supposed to do. For an extended season of my life, I could not do what I had been called to do. I wasn't doing ministry. And although I was grateful that God provided a soft place for me to land, what I was doing just wasn't my calling. It really wasn't what I *cared* to do.

But it was what I *could* do. Was I thrilled to be there? Not even in the least. Most mornings, during those four long years, I'd hide my face in my hands and wonder, *God, is there still a place for me? You're not through with me, are you?*

But then I would dry my eyes—and go right back to building the very best bricks I could! A lot of people stuck in a Small World seem to say, "This may be where God wants me right now, and it is something I can, in fact, do. But what I want to know is, isn't there something *else* I can do?"

I've learned that whatever is in front of you right now is exactly what God has for you to do . . . right now. So just do it with all your heart! Even if it's stacking bricks, stack 'em with a vengeance!

Whatever is in front of you right now is exactly what God has for you to do . . . right now. So just do it with all your heart!

If you'll give it your whole heart and commit yourself to it, pouring yourself out with absolute abandon, then . . . when God wants you doing something else, you won't be stacking stones anymore. No, you'll be doing the very thing you've always wanted to do. And you'll scratch your head in amazement, wondering, *How did I get here?*

You will have gotten here because God delivered you.

However, if you waste all your time groaning because "God hasn't opened the door," then you become the primary reason for God's deliverance being delayed!

So if you're gonna build bricks anyway, why not build the best bricks you can? That's what the Israelites did. They built huge structures they cared nothing about. And every single course was paving God's eventual pathway to Israel's promised deliverance!

FROM BUILDING BRICKS TO MAKING A BABY

But there's another response that only *one* Israelite did. Oh, I'm sure my hero also did her share of groaning. I'm equally confident she struggled to forge that mental toughness that eventually empowered her to take her heartache directly to God. And she stayed at the task—an extremely *undesirable* task—day after backbreaking day.

But in addition (and in spite of a relentless oppression), Jochebed decided to have a baby. Some would call him an ill-timed baby. But bad timing or not, this was one blessed fetus. Because his mama did something for him that nobody else in Goshen ever did.

Right in the middle of a ghetto called Goshen, a little Hebrew boy was born. And his mama "saw that he was a fine child" (2:2). She took one look at her baby and said, "Isn't he beautiful?"

Of course, *every* parent thinks that. Meanwhile everybody else is thinking, *Looks like an overgrown raisin to me.* But Jochebed's assessment was more than maternal prejudice. In the New Testament, when Stephen recounted this story, he said that when Moses was born, it was obvious he was "no ordinary child" (Acts 7:20). Jochebed perceived, from the sheer beauty of this kid, that he was going to be powerfully used by God. So she did something nobody else dared do: "she hid him for three months" (Exodus 2:2).

That may not sound like a big deal, but they were living in tiny, paper-thin shanties that were literally stacked right up against each other. Besides that, the Egyptians sent nightly patrols through Goshen, spying out any crying babies who hadn't yet been killed. And let's face it, newborns aren't exactly quiet!

Yet my hero pulled it off. She hid her baby for three months. How did she muster the courage? "By faith Moses' parents hid him for three months . . . , because they saw he was no ordinary child, and they were not afraid of the king's edict" (Hebrews 11:23).

Mark that. Especially if you groan because our culture is so polluted. Despite year after year of Israel's constant exposure to Egypt's pagan value system, Jochebed and her husband, Amram, stood strong and remained unswervingly faithful to God. She feared God more than she feared Pharaoh. So you see, it *is* possible!

SHE ACTED IN HOPE

When she couldn't hide the boy any longer, my hero built a bassinet, lined it with pitch, and then set her son afloat among the bulrushes in the very cove where Pharaoh's daughter was sure to find him (see Exodus 2:3).

That's not what she *wanted* to do. She wanted to raise her boy—in her home, on her terms, according to her values. But since she couldn't do what she wanted to do, she determined to do what God was giving her to do now . . . she built a floating bassinet.

With strong mental toughness, Jochebed may have researched *where* the princess bathed and *when* she bathed. Then she nestled her bundle securely among the reeds, rehearsed her preteen daughter, Miriam, as she recited her crucial lines, and then went home to pace the floor, groan, and of course, cry out to God!

That boat was Jochebed's illogical act of unbridled hope. Why assume Pharaoh's daughter would do anything other than just nudge Moses' raft right on down the river? Moses was just one of thousands of Hebrew babies who took that sad trip. But somehow Moses' mama knew it wasn't going to go that way. So instead of slumping in despair, instead of just handing baby Moses over to die, Jochebed acted in hope!

I agree with Freda Crews when she said, "Hope sets in motion the belief that things can change."[4] And sure enough, once Jochebed's hope was set in motion, things changed very quickly.

"Pharaoh's daughter went down to the Nile to bathe, and . . . she saw the basket among the reeds. . . . She opened it and saw the baby. He was crying, and she felt sorry for him. 'This is one of the Hebrew babies,' she said" (vv. 5, 6).

That's when Miriam, seeing her compassionate response, darted out from her hiding place and asked, "Shall I go and get one of the Hebrew women to nurse the baby for you?" (v. 7). Brilliant! Miriam pretended she was just passing by, but then she casually said, "I can try to find somebody to help, if you'd like."

Once Jochebed's hope was set in motion, things changed very quickly.

For three months, mama and Miriam had rehearsed this moment—so when the moment finally arrived, it was breathtaking. The princess actually said, "Yes, go." Then Miriam "went and got the baby's mother" (v. 8).

When Jochebed arrived, Pharaoh's daughter said, "Take this baby and nurse him for me, and I will pay you" (v. 9). Is that cool or what? Not only was her baby's life miraculously spared, mama got to raise him! Even more, she got *paid*!

MORE THAN ENOUGH TIME

It's so easy, isn't it, to whine about our world and think, *There's no way we can raise godly kids today. We're outmanned. The forces are too great!*

But the story of Jochebed stands as God's forever reminder that there is *always* hope, that you are *never* alone. And that you need never fear defeat. This woman was dirt poor. She had nothing going for her but her own relentless diligence—and the power of God. Yet she saved her baby and then got paid to raise him.

How long did she have him? We don't know. The Bible merely says, "When the child grew older, she took him to Pharaoh's daughter" (v. 10). Many scholars believe this was a longer period than just till he was weaned. Some suggest Jochebed had her boy for as long as five years. Whatever time she had, she did more than just nurse that kid.

She flowed into his life with the same fervent drive that empowered her to build that boat in the first place. Every day she reminded young Moses, "Honey, God saved you for a special purpose. Look around—you don't see any other Hebrew boys your age, do you? You're it. The only one. And since God promised our nation a deliverer . . . I think you might just be him!"

Then she taught him about Abraham and Isaac and Jacob and Joseph. She had only a few short years to mold that boy into a man of God. Could she cram enough truth into a preschooler's heart so that, as he grew up in Egypt's palaces, he'd still be able to keep his eyes trained on God?

It was more than enough. Hebrews 11:24 says, "By faith Moses, when he had grown up, refused to be known as the son of Pharaoh's daughter." After having been raised in the palace, after having been trained in Egypt's finest schools, and after having been thoroughly immersed in all things Egyptian, why would Moses walk away from royalty?

"He chose to be mistreated along with the people of God rather than to enjoy the pleasures of sin for a short time. He regarded disgrace for the sake of Christ as of greater value than the treasures of Egypt" (vv. 25, 26).

Now . . . where do you suppose, in all that boy's vast education, he had learned about the Messiah? On his mama's knee, that's where. Moses' mama, my hero, had only a few years while stuck in the sewage of an anti-god system that has rarely been equaled in history. Yet though she groaned, by faith she also stayed at the task. And when Moses had grown into manhood, by faith he also chose to be faithful . . . just like mama (see v. 27).

JOCHEBED'S ARMY

Just like Jochebed, you don't have the luxury of depending on our culture to help underscore what you're teaching your kids. But Jochebed's legacy is a lasting one—you can still get the job done.

Groan if you need to. Cry if you must. And then after you've sighed, get with it. Get back to building your baby's boat. Get back to seizing every teachable moment, especially in those early years. Faithfully and systematically teach your children the things of God. Read to them from Bible storybooks. Enroll them in children's ministries. Model before them your own faith and good works.

As Moses himself would later say, "Impress [God's commandments] on your children. Talk about them when you sit at home and when you walk along the road, when you lie down and when you get up" (Deuteronomy 6:7).

You don't have to preach at them; just keep it real. But remain vigilant. Seize every ordinary opportunity and employ every unexpected encounter as another chance to point your kids to Jesus.

And that's why Jochebed is my hero. She delivered a helpless little baby—then nurtured him to stay afloat despite the angry waves of a seductively pagan culture. Her influence ultimately helped empower him to do a bit of delivering of his own. Can't you hear it:

"What a great plan, Moses! Where'd you come up with that?"

"From my mom."

The authorities still aren't sure why it happened. By every account, the takeoff from Detroit's Metro Airport was routine that day in 1987.[5] Winds were moderate, the pilots were veterans, and the plane had already been in service once that day.

Yet as the aircraft lifted off the runway, it was clear that something terrible was about to happen. Eyewitnesses watched in horror as the loaded plane staggered into the sky, failed to gain altitude, grazed a light pole in a car-rental lot, and then slammed into the highway, breaking apart as it skidded. The wreckage was almost immediately engulfed in flames.

Seize every ordinary opportunity and employ every unexpected encounter as another chance to point your kids to Jesus.

The crash of Flight 255 was one of the worst in U.S. history. One hundred fifty-six people died in the resulting inferno. The blaze was so enormous, the heat so intense, that no survivors were expected to be found.

Miraculously, rescuers found four-year-old Cecelia Cichan badly burned but alive! How did she survive while every other passenger was killed? One story that was widely circulated (but later revealed as not true) was that her mother had sheltered her from the blast with her own body. As it turns out, the only explanation for Cecelia's survival is the gracious intervention of God.

We would have considered Cecelia's mother a hero had her charred remains become the wall of protection that sustained little Cecelia's life. We admire parents willing to take risks for their children. While God's intervention is often required to save a child, his first plan is that godly parents stand in the gap for their children—both physically and spiritually.

Mom and dad, you are called by God to be your child's wall of protection. We live in a crazy world where wrong is affirmed as right, where the good feel shame and the evil express pride. Your kids need *you* to be their spiritual heroes. They need your protective care, your instruction, and your shelter.

And if they don't get it, then apart from God's intervention they might not survive the blast . . . after all.

07

SAME HOUSE
BUT NOT THE
SAME PAGE

1 Samuel 1:19-25; 2:11-17; 3:1-18

PEOPLE LIKE YOU

Kathy grew up in a strict family. Her parents expected her to believe what they believed. But as she grew older, she began to take her own path. She grew in her ego strength and her ability to debate ideas with her parents and other authority figures. This, of course, brought consequences. She became at odds with her parents, which was often evidenced in loud arguments. This led into other unacceptable behaviors all around. It took Kathy's moving out of the home and going off to college to shake the anxiety from her daily life.

When parents and children find themselves on different pages (spiritually, ideologically, intellectually, behaviorally, or emotionally), it can be a very unsettling experience. Most parents make the mistake of going into control mode to corral their children's ideas into their own liking. This only creates resentment and further distance in the relationship. Some parents go the opposite way, allowing their children to think (and behave) however they want. This is just as damaging, if not worse.

So there is a large gray area between indoctrination and self-determination. It takes much communication and openness on both sides. We were all given free will, but God also provided children with parents to teach them his ways.

I once heard a story about a high school football team and their archrival. At this point in the season, they were the only unbeaten teams in the state; but after the game, only one of them would remain unbeaten. So before boarding the team bus, the coach had the squad lie down on the gym floor and, for more than half an hour, just stare at the ceiling in complete darkness and silence. He wanted them to find their game faces. He wanted them to get mentally tough so they'd storm onto the field and put some serious pads on some people. Finally, the coach quietly said, "All right, no one make a sound—not even a word. Just get on the bus."

That team played the game of a lifetime that night, absolutely destroying their opponent. After the ride back to their school and an impromptu pep rally in the parking lot, the team conducted their own celebration in the locker room—everybody that is, except the quarterback. He was so moved by their wide margin of victory that he slipped into the gym to be alone for a while.

There was a body lying in the middle of the gym. Talk about spooky! The quarterback walked over, but the body didn't move. So he gingerly tapped the body with his foot. It was one of the other players, number 42. When the quarterback touched him, he shot to his feet and shouted, "Yeah! All right, let's go!!"

Evidently, number 42 had been partying the night before. And when he lay down for the pregame preparation, he also passed out! He had been asleep for hours, missing the biggest game of his life!

Samuel, the focus of this chapter, was also asleep . . . until he received a strange, thoroughly life-changing wake-up call.

Truth is, *all* of Israel, God's chosen people, had fallen asleep spiritually. Many years had passed since Moses led them to the promised land. And still more years would pass before the glory days of King David. As the book of 1 Samuel opens, there are no heavy-duty wars worth recording, no vicious famines that threatened ... just a restful interlude filled mostly with calm and peace. The Israelites had fallen into a deep, spiritual complacency. Even their religious leaders started phoning it in, as the whole nation approached God (and the things of God) with a very ho-hum, lackadaisical attitude.

Everybody that is, except young Samuel. He alone remained diligent as he "ministered before the LORD under Eli. In those days the word of the LORD was rare; there were not many visions" (1 Samuel 3:1).

In other words, God was mostly silent. There was no consistent message from him and no faithful instruction coming from the priests of God. It was a very sleepy, spiritually lazy time. But not sleepy for long ...

THE WAKE-UP CALL

"One night Eli, whose eyes were becoming so weak that he could barely see, was lying down in his usual place. The lamp of God had not yet gone out, and Samuel was lying down in the temple of the LORD, where the ark of God was" (vv. 2, 3).

A key fixture in Israel's tabernacle was a holy place where the instruments of worship were stored. Among these artifacts was the menorah, a lamp that, according to Moses' law, was never to go out. The priests serving in the tabernacle took turns sleeping near the holy place so they could trim the wick and replenish the oil as needed. Evidently, that night was Samuel's rotation. He slept in, essentially, a closet. And that's when it happened.

"The LORD called Samuel. Samuel [awakened and] answered, 'Here I am'" (v. 4).

When nobody responded, "he ran to Eli and said, 'Here I am; you called me.' But Eli said, 'I did not call; go back and lie down'" (v. 5). So he did.

"Again the LORD called, 'Samuel!' And Samuel got up and went to Eli and said, 'Here I am; you called me.'

"'My son,' Eli said, 'I did not call; go back and lie down'" (v. 6).

Our inspired narrator adds some clarification: "Now Samuel did not yet know the LORD: The word of the LORD had not yet been revealed to him" (v. 7).

Back before people had the Scriptures, a record of the written Word of God, God broke his silence by speaking audibly to a prophet or giving direction to someone of his choosing through a supernatural encounter. But since God and Samuel weren't yet on speaking terms, everything Samuel knew about God had come through Eli, not his own personal experience. Obviously Samuel was confused. So he did the only thing he knew to do: he went to Eli.

Let's linger here a minute. Samuel faithfully ministered before the Lord. He spent all day every day learning about him. He was in the same house where God lived . . . but not yet on the same page.

A MOM WHO WOULD NOT BE DENIED

Rewinding a little . . . evidently Samuel's mama, Hannah, couldn't get pregnant. She regularly visited the temple, and she spent the majority of her time there begging God to give her a son. She even cut a deal with God: "O LORD Almighty, if you will only look upon your servant's misery and remember me, and not forget your servant but give her a son, then I will give him [back to you] for all the days of his life" (1:11).

And that's how Samuel came to be born.

True to Hannah's word, "after he was weaned, she took the boy with her . . . and brought him to the house of the LORD" (v. 24).

We can't track the exact chronology, so Samuel might've

been three years old . . . or perhaps a tad older than that. What we *do* know is, the only reason this kid was even born was because his mama relentlessly and tenaciously prayed. She grabbed the horns of the altar and pleaded with God to help her get pregnant!

Being a mom is a calling. I'm in the ministry primarily because God gave me a godly mom who prays. A mom who prays can bring about a calling-down kind of power on her kids that the world may never fully appreciate. Sadly, the cultural disposition of our day is that motherhood isn't significant. If you say, "I'm a mom," it's almost laughable— because moms don't get their just due.

Since God and Samuel weren't yet on speaking terms, everything Samuel knew about God had come through Eli.

Samuel's birth began in the heart of a praying woman who cried out to God for a baby. And then, having birthed that baby, she cared for him—and flowed into his life (much like Jochebed did with Moses). Then she took Samuel to Pastor Eli and said, "You take it from here!"

You don't have to be the next Billy Graham to be a person of influence—just be the next Billy Graham's mama. And who knows, maybe God has uniquely positioned you to do exactly that. It could happen, because there is enormous power in a godly mama who prays, who takes her job seriously, and who stays at the task . . . no matter what.

CULTIVATE THE TASTE

One of the most misinterpreted verses in the Bible is Proverbs 22:6, where King Solomon made a wonderful promise to every mom and dad: "Train a child in the way he should go, and when he is old he will not turn from it."

Here's a typical interpretation of that verse: "Mom and dad, be sure little Joel attends church every Sunday. And teach him to say grace at mealtimes and pray before bedtime. Give him Scripture to memorize and pack him off to Christian camp each summer. If you can, send him to Christian school, or better yet, instruct him in your home. And when he's a teenager, make sure he's plugged into youth group. You do that, and when Joel grows up, he may go through some rebellion—he may even sow some wild oats—but when he gets old enough, he'll stop that foolishness ... and come back to God!"

That interpretation really isn't all that encouraging, is it? What kind of promise is that anyway, if all it means is that when little Joel gets broken down and decrepit, he'll come hobbling back to God?

Not only is that interpretation not encouraging, it's not accurate either. That's not God's big promise for struggling parents! When Proverbs 22:6 says "train a child," it means to "create an appetite," to "cultivate the taste." Most people think the word *train* here means "discipline." So we parents tend to adopt a boot-camp strategy where we drill our kids to toe the line and salute crisply to our strictly designed spiritual regimen.

Force-feeding doesn't cut it—not when it's beets, and especially not when it's spiritual truth.

But that's not what Solomon had in mind.

That word *train* (*chanak* in Hebrew) actually means "palate, the roof of the mouth." It could be used to describe our sense of taste and the pleasure of having honey on the tongue. It was also used to describe the actions of a midwife who, soon after helping deliver a child, would dip her own finger into the juice of crushed dates and massage the baby's palate in order to create that baby's sensation for sucking. Then his mother would begin to nurse him.[1]

Solomon's message is not: Parents, make sure your kids get with the program. It's: Parents, your job is to cultivate within your kids an instinctive taste for the spiritual things of God. It's not about "Do as I say!" Neither is it a strict legalism that demands some predetermined response. It's the loving, ongoing process of developing in your kids a thirst for God.

Admittedly, in those early years you can ram a lot of religion down Junior's throat—and he pretty much has to take it. I remember strapping our kids into the high chair . . . and because even then they hated spinach and beets, I would find fiendish delight in hiding the beets under some applesauce. They thought they were getting the good stuff, but I tricked 'em!

That may work for a while, but in time, force-feeding doesn't cut it—not when it's beets, and especially not when it's spiritual truth. A lot of adults are still in spiritual rebellion today simply because their well-meaning parents strapped them into their church seats and forced them to eat what they never taught them to love.

Solomon was essentially saying, "Parents, this is a wonderful promise. But only if you're willing to positively cultivate your children's taste for God. You do that, and they'll walk with God for a lifetime!"

IRRESPONSIBLE FATHERHOOD

Since Hannah had only three or four years with Samuel, was it enough? Did her spiritual values make the transfer to become the values of her son? As a matter of fact, they did. Although he still hadn't connected all the dots, Samuel obviously had a strong thirst for God.

That tells you something about the inherent power of a godly parent. Childhood development experts tend to agree that the most formative years of a child's life are between birth and age three. When it comes to how kids connect with their parents—and how they respond to their leadership—the bulk of the job is already done before Junior hits kindergarten.

Samuel was so heavily impacted by his mama—and his taste for God already implanted in his heart—that there was very little his less-than-ideal living conditions could do to negate what mama had already done. The temple environment was not at all what it should've been. For one thing, Eli's vision was failing (1 Samuel 3:2)—physically because of his age, but also spiritually because Eli had lost his edge.

Maybe he stayed in the game too long, or maybe his heart was never fully engaged. Whatever the reason, nothing leaks quite like vision. And Israel's spiritual leader (who should've had a firm grasp on things) had instead become passive, complacent, and uninvolved.

Nowhere was that more obvious than in his own family. Eli's sons were "scoundrels who had no respect for the LORD" (2:12, *NLT*). They were so spiritually callous, in fact, that they grabbed a meat hook, swiped it through the pot where people were offering their sacrifices to God, and whatever meat their hook grabbed, they took home and served for dinner! This sin "was very serious in the LORD's sight, for they treated the LORD's offerings with contempt" (v. 17, *NLT*).

If you think *that's* bad, listen to this: "Eli, who was very old, heard about everything his sons were doing . . . and how they slept with the women who served at . . . the Tent of Meeting" (v. 22). In other words, these associate priests took sexual advantage of the women who were volunteering at their church! And they did it . . . inside the church! And Eli knew about it!

Sure he was old, but he was a man of God before he ever

was those two boys' daddy. And by law, those two scoundrels were supposed to be dragged to the edge of town and stoned to death! (see Leviticus 24:13-16). Instead, all this daddy could muster was, "[*Now boys,*] why do you do such things?" (1 Samuel 2:23).

Do you realize you can lead your child into sin simply by doing nothing?

◆ You're too busy to monitor your son's activities.
◆ You have no clue who your daughter is dating or what she does on those dates.
◆ You can't remember the last time you discussed issues related to morality and decency with your kids.

And then when your kids wind up with a serious problem with drugs, pornography, sexual promiscuity, or stealing—behavior most people would consider a red flag—you just close your eyes and hope the crisis will somehow resolve itself.

One night on our way home from shopping, Cindy and I drove by McDonald's. Cindy noticed that our son Drew (normally working inside) was outside.

She wanted to go toward him, but I said: "Let's hang back a second."

Drew was on his break. But since we had been dealing with some stuff, I wanted to see what he would do. Sure enough, he started doing something he knew he wasn't supposed to do. So I jammed the accelerator, and we drove to within inches of where he was standing.

That led to stain number one in Drew's underpants.

Then I got out of the truck and told him to get into the truck.

That created stain number two.

A few minutes and several strong words later, we set our hostage free—and as we drove away, we both laughed out loud! (I know it sounds cruel.) Do you know why we laughed?

Because we are so grateful that God is on our team! That encounter was an incredible teaching moment for our son.

Yet Eli just looked the other way. Or even worse, uttered some pansied little whimper: "Why are you doing that?"

Sometime later, God said to Samuel, "I told [Eli] that I would judge his family . . . because of the sin he knew about . . . [yet] he failed to restrain them" (3:13). Please note that his boys committed the sin, but because Eli refused to address it, God held *him* accountable for it too. Bottom line: Eli didn't want the hassle. And it *is* a hassle to deal with bad behavior!

STAY THE COURSE

When Solomon said, "Train up a child," the meaning wasn't limited to a narrow age group, like toddlers. In 1 Samuel 4:21 this word for *child* describes an infant. In 1 Samuel 1:27 it describes a youngster who's been weaned. In Genesis 21:16 it describes Ishmael in his teens, and in Genesis 37:2 it describes Joseph at age seventeen. Genesis 34:19 uses the same word for a young man about to get married.

So this word for *child* is a very broad term. The implication is clear: if you want to claim this promise for your children, you've got to dedicate yourself to the ongoing (some might say never-ending) process of training. Your job may begin in the cradle, but it doesn't end until your children are safely launched into adulthood.

It is your God-given duty to keep one eye constantly glued on your kids—watching and observing them, spending time with them. You must thoroughly inspect their hearts and rigorously gauge their hormones, regularly adjusting your training—adapting, retooling, and sensitively responding with just the right approach that will keep feeding their still-much-to-be-desired taste for God.

Eli didn't do that. He tried instead to be his boys' big

STUCK IN A SMALL WORLD

buddy. He was afraid he might lose them if he came on too strong; so he tried to win them over by being permissive. But listen to God's take on Eli's passive parenting. He asked Eli, "Why do you honor your sons more than me?" (1 Samuel 2:29).

Hannah's little boy lived in the temple, a place you'd think was a spiritual safe place; yet this temple was anything but safe. But even there God had a purpose. It's just that Samuel had no clue what that purpose might be.

God's Story in You

As we make our way through Small World, not even one family escapes unscathed. On every family tree we find brokenness, rebellion, and unfaithfulness; yet when it happens to us, we all wonder, *Why is this happening to us?* We ask because we view our Small World through the lens of our own finite experience. Since we're limited to that miniscule frame, none of what we're enduring seems to makes sense—especially when we mistakenly believe the story being written is *our* story.

His boys committed the sin, but because Eli refused to address it, God held *him* accountable for it too.

It's not. Your life is not the story of you. It's the story of God's transforming work ... *in* you. You have a part to play in the drama God has chosen for you—but *the* central character of this story is God, not you.

I heard someone say, "God is writing an epic story in your life, but he tells his epic in epochs."

Those two words (*epic* and *epoch*) sound essentially the same, but their meanings are dramatically different. An epic is a story portraying larger-than-life adventures that cover an extended period of time; whereas, an epoch is just one small story, an event within the larger story. It's a snapshot rather than a full-length feature film.

We see our life in epochs—and that's why we don't understand. Not being able to see the bigger picture is the problem.

His mom constantly repeated, "Don't try to change him; just love him."

Think back. God made an epic promise to Abraham, that he would father a great nation (Genesis 12:2). But the only part of that story Abraham saw was Isaac and Ishmael constantly fighting each other. Isaac also was privy to just one epoch within God's grander epic. He had no clue that of his son Jacob's twelve sons, one of those twelve would be used by God to build that great nation.

Abraham and Isaac could only see God's epic unfold in epochs, barely more than just one frame at a time.

We can read and try to believe that God "works out everything in conformity with the purpose of his will" (Ephesians 1:11), but because God's grand epic unfolds one page at a time, it's not always clear. It's hard to see why God allows you to slog through stuff in order to produce within you certain character traits. And only later do you realize, *Were it not for* that *tough encounter, I'd never be equipped for* this *encounter.*

That's why the Bible says, "Give thanks in all circumstances" (1 Thessalonians 5:18). God's epic unfolds in epochs. You have no clue what he might be doing, but he's already using this current difficulty to build within you the strength you're going to need for next year's challenge.

Most of the time we pray, "God, make this stop! I want

my son to come around ... now! I want this ugly relationship healed ... today! God, why won't you answer me?"

Samuel had his questions too. He wanted to be with his mom but lived, instead, with a passive old priest and his two carnal sons—and he had *no* idea why.

Just Doin' Church

Samuel did the only thing he did know: temple protocol. Samuel knew how to do church, so he "ministered before the LORD"(1 Samuel 2:11) even though—as we've already seen—Samuel did not yet know God but merely had a taste.

Oh, but he *did* know how to light the altar of incense and which sacrifices were offered at which feasts. He even knew about the drink offerings, the meal offerings, and the ceremonial washings. Why, this kid even knew all about the cleansing ashes of the red heifer! (see Numbers 19:1-10). Samuel knew how to do church—but he did not know God.

Chad knew how to do church too. He gave his life to Christ when he was just twelve. He knew all the church songs, he knew when to take Communion, when to stand, and when to sit down. He had church protocol down cold.

But then he began to darken right before his parents' eyes. His hairstyle changed, he got some piercings, and started wearing dark clothing. Then his grades tanked. He and his girlfriend were arrested for smoking grass. That led to even more serious brushes with the law and, ultimately, jail time.

His parents, both believers, tried to love him through his epoch. His mom constantly repeated, "Don't try to change him; just love him." And she did—even when he ridiculed her, saying, "How can you be *so* stupid to believe that Jesus stuff?"

But how could this terrible thing have happened? Chad knew what to do during meet-and-greet time, he knew how to find Psalms in his pew Bible ...

When my daughter Andrea was in kindergarten, she said, "Daddy! Guess what? I learned the Pledge o' Legiance! And I can say the whole thing by heart."

I knew she wanted me to, so I said, "Say it for me!"

"Sure! But I don't want no help."

"*Any* help."

"Huh?"

"Never mind."

She cleared her throat, stood straight and tall, and said: "I pledge legiance to the flag, of the Nited States of Merica. And to the public for whichit stans, one nation, under God, innadabizibible. With liverty and justin for all. Please be seated."

Then she sat down!

I said, "Say it again!"

And again, she included the tag line: "Please be seated."

My daughter's Pledge was one line longer than the rest of America thinks it is! She learned by rote memory what her teacher had said. Experts tell us that rote is the lowest form of learning, because all you do is memorize. You bypass comprehension and just stuff random information into your skull.

The same thing can happen in church. We teach our kids lines from the Bible, and they rattle them off without ever making the slightest personal application. We help them master the lingo and church protocol without ever cultivating within them a genuine taste for God. Our kids ingest just enough data about Jesus and have just enough exposure to know how to do church. We effectively immunize them from ever getting the real disease.

PREPPED FOR HEARING GOD

The good news is that Samuel still had the taste his mama had given him. He still hungered for an authentic and soul-nourishing connection with God. So even in the midst of rank hypocrisy, Samuel kept serving . . . anyway.

That's when the voice called out and awakened Samuel from his slumber. After the voice spoke a third time, "Eli realized that the LORD was calling the boy" (3:8).

His vision was dim, and he'd made plenty of mistakes—but Eli could still recognize a God moment when it happened. So he told Samuel, "'Go and lie down, and if he calls you, say, 'Speak, LORD, for your servant is listening.' So Samuel went and lay down in his place. The LORD came [again] . . . , calling as at the other times, 'Samuel! Samuel!' Then Samuel said, 'Speak, for your servant is listening.' And the LORD said to Samuel: 'See, I am about to do something in Israel that will make the ears of everyone who hears of it tingle'" (vv. 9-11).

What would make those Hebrew ears tingle was a judgment against Eli that God had already warned Eli would happen if things didn't change. Eli and his family would be destroyed—and Samuel would become Israel's new priest.

Another interpretation of Proverbs 22:6 is that parents are to train a child in keeping with his individual bent. Parents, as they fulfill their parenting assignments, should take into account each child's individuality and inclination. That doesn't mean they let him do whatever he pleases. It means they adapt to his God-given temperament, his unique giftedness, and his perceived ability.

The surest way to raise a rebel is to raise him *your* way, make him a carbon copy of you, or try to make him excel in ways you never could yourself. That's what too many of us do. We decide the way our kids should go! "After all, I'm the parent; I know what's best for my kid."

So we dive in . . . with the latest parenting manual in one hand and our own particular biases and hang-ups in the other. But then we wind up either parenting the way our parents did—or the exact opposite way.

In my coaching days with Josh's Little League baseball team, I coached a kid whose dad had never been an athlete. But he wanted Junior to be one. I remember when they brought Junior's new bat to practice. It was a full-size, 34-inch, 30-ounce bat. Not even Barry Bonds could swing that thing—even after steroids! (Not that he ever *used* steroids.) But Junior was carrying an even heavier burden than that bat—he was also saddled with the pressure to become what his daddy could never be!

We wind up either parenting the way our parents did—or the exact opposite way.

Raising your kids your way will never get the job done! If you insist on doing it your way, your relationship will be marked by threats and humiliation, plus loads of resentment and hostility. And one day, if you never learn to train your son in his own way . . . if you never learn to appreciate your daughter for the person God made her to be . . . the time will come when all you'll have between you are grunts and groans. Your relationship will erode to the point that one day your kids will thumb their noses at everything you stand for—even your faith.

NEVER TOO LATE TO CHANGE

Eli blew it with his kids big time. They were grown, married, and raising hellions of their own. But God gave Eli another chance . . . with Samuel.

What's the first thing Eli did with that chance? Instead of making his sons the only ones in need of a diagnosis, he took a very painful, internal look and made a most troubling self-diagnosis: "I blew it with my boys. I failed to lead them with tender strength and a firm, loving hand. I was more afraid of losing them than I was of displeasing God."

Since only God knows what he had in mind when he created you, finding *him* is the only way you will ever find *you*.

Samuel's mama had first helped him cultivate a thirst for God. And Eli made a crucial mid-course correction—and then stayed at the task and carefully guided Samuel according to Samuel's own way. And when Samuel finally heard God's voice, he not only found out who *God* was, he discovered who *he* was too!

Children need a safe place to find out who they are. As they grow in their own awareness of God—and then come to actually acknowledge him—that's when they finally realize, *I know who I am too!*

◆ I am loved by God!

◆ I am more than a conqueror through Christ!

◆ I am in control of my life (and no longer being controlled *by* life)!

The bottom line of Samuel's gripping story is: you cannot know who you are until you find out who God is. And since only God knows what he had in mind when he created you, finding *him* is the only way you will ever find *you*.

Wise is the parent who says, "Sweetie, money can't define you. And hangin' with the popular crowd won't define you either. And even marking your body and wearing certain clothes . . . that can't define who you are. Oh, I understand why you do it. When I was your age, I'd do just about anything to fit in too. But I've learned that the beginning of wisdom is learning to be comfortable with being different from your crowd. I'm talking about you being you!"

WHAT DEFINES YOU

Some people are clones primarily because they don't yet know who they are. My generation did the same thing with long hair and tie-dyed T-shirts and peace signs big enough to choke a horse. And we did it for the same reason teens today do it—to be different.

But not even *different* can define you. Only knowing God can define you. When you finally get to the point where you don't care what anybody thinks or what the crowd wants you to do—simply because you know who God is (which means you also know who *you* are)—that's when you start listening to a truly different voice, a voice you know can fully define you.

Has something like that ever happened to you? Have you ever felt you were absolutely encountering the magnitude of God? Have you ever so sensed his eternal purpose for you that you radically and thoroughly released your will to his will and your heart to his heart?

That's what was happening to Samuel right now. God was raising up a new order, a fresh generation of sold-out God-followers, a brand-new army of warriors who could recognize God's voice and who were wholeheartedly dedicated to God's purpose.

This group is still seeking recruits today, still looking for young men and women who aren't afraid of what anybody else thinks or says. They're listening to *the* voice . . . and nothing will ever cause them to turn back.

Proverbs 22:6 ends with a promise: "Train a child in the way he should go, and when he is old he will not turn from it." The word *old* here simply means "hair on the chin" or "bearded one." So this promise is not about some ninety-year-old prodigal hobbling back home after a lifetime of deviancy; this is a young man just starting to shave.

God's promise means that if you'll cultivate an early

spiritual thirst in each child and then faithfully stay at the task, and if you'll train your child according to his divinely appointed personality . . . when he grows to maturity, he will not rebel. He'll keep right on walking just as you have taught him.

Now that's what I call a promise . . . after all.

08

PAYING
DAD'S
TAB

2 Samuel 11–18

➡️ PEOPLE LIKE YOU

Tom had all the marks of success in his day: possessions, financial security, notoriety, and accomplishments. Everything but success at home. He had chosen a trade-off. He had opted to sacrifice his relationship with his wife and his children—as well as the influence he would have upon his children—by being gone. He was not at their ball games or recitals. He was not there when they had a hard day and needed someone to listen. He was not there physically or emotionally when something traumatic happened in their lives. And when they needed him most, he did not know them or understand them.

Quality time only happens when *quantity* time has been in place. Tom felt empty but didn't know why.

What Tom did not realize was how his trade-off would affect his children. They had no positive role model for what a husband or father should look like. When his daughters went looking for boyfriends, they did not choose wisely—partly because they were trying to fill up the hole in their hearts left by dad. When his sons became husbands, they did not know how to be one, other than by being selfish. And when any of them became parents, since their view of what parenting looked like was skewed, they did the same thing they had seen while growing up.

"I can't do it, Daddy."

She looked at me with a sad face that could melt even the stoutest father's heart.

"Come on, Jess. You *can* do it. Just put your crutches down on the first step and then slowly lower your good leg till you feel the carpet between your toes."

We'd just come home from the hospital, and my daughter was learning to transport herself with the help of crutches. Her right leg was plastered from toe to hip, and her blue eyes were wide with fear. There we stood, at the top step in our home, as Jessica faced a challenge that is by any measure a frightening journey.

"Why don't you just carry me down, Daddy?"

She already knew my answer. With twelve long weeks of recovery, if she didn't learn how to get around, she would soon be one bored, totally isolated puppy dog. Like it or not, Jessica had to learn to do steps.

"But Daddy, I'm afraid I'll fall."

A legitimate fear, no doubt. If you've ever descended a flight of stairs with only one good leg and two awkward crutches, you know how tough those steps can be. And knowing my daughter, I knew Jessica had already mentally envisioned her mangled body crumpled in a bloody heap at the bottom of the stairs.

So I said, "Jess, I'm standing right in front of you. If you even look like you're gonna fall, I will catch you. You will not get hurt. I'm here for you. And I will protect you every step of the way."

"Do you promise, Daddy?"

That's a question every child wants answered. And whether the query is verbally expressed or is the silent cry of a searching heart, every son and every daughter from every culture, every tribe, and every nation on this spinning mud ball needs to know whether daddy can be trusted.

◆ "If I take a tumble, will you be there to catch me?"

◆ "Do you mean it, Daddy?"

◆ "You're not gonna walk out on me, are you?"

◆ "You'll be there for me when I need you, right?"

◆ "Do you really love me?"

A DAD ON THE CLIMB

As we continue our voyage through Small World, we encounter a world-famous, lavishly wealthy, and politically successful king—a godly man who modeled before his people an unbridled passion for the worship of God. Yet King David as a dad just couldn't be trusted.

Politically, he was a juggernaut—a brilliant organizer, a gifted strategist, and an awe-inspiring leader. Under his rule, David's armies conquered Israel's enemies; he expanded Israel's borders, and he established key trade relationships throughout the entire world.

Personally, David was a ticking time bomb. With each new alliance he formed with foreign powers, he married and then brought into the palace yet another new wife. By my count, he had eight wives who are named in Scripture, several who aren't named, plus a few random live-in lovers.

For simplicity, let's estimate that he had somewhere in the vicinity of two dozen "wives," and with them there came the potential for even more kiddos than that! At least a dozen rugrats are named for us, but it's a good bet David had fathered at least three times that number.

But even twelve would be too many for this already overcommitted dad. After fulfilling his kingly assignments each day, how much time and energy do you think David had left to invest in two dozen wives plus enough kids to fill their own school bus?

Yet . . . there's not much evidence he even tried. David afforded himself the intense pleasure involved in *making* babies but did not avail himself enough in the inconvenience of *raising* the babies he made.

We can clearly hear King David's family bomb ticking one night when he was strolling on his rooftop. He spied a woman taking a bath. Intrigued, David called for her, she came, and they slept together. He thought he'd gotten away with it. There was just one problem: Bathsheba got pregnant.

Like a hot knife through butter, Nathan's words pierced David's heart.

David tried to cover his tracks by bringing her hubby back from the war so he could sleep with her too. David got Uriah drunk, but even a drunk Uriah had more class than David. He refused to enjoy the pleasure of lovemaking as long as his troops were still in harm's way.

So David thought he had no choice ... but to murder the guy! Then he married Bathsheba. Sometime later their baby was born—and only David and Bathsheba knew the truth.

Oh ... and God too, of course. "The thing David had done displeased the LORD" (2 Samuel 11:27). God sent a weather-beaten prophet named Nathan to confront him. Nathan began by telling a story about two men. One man was rich and had a large flock of sheep, while the other was poor and had just one little lamb. The rich man was entertaining guests for dinner; but instead of choosing their meal from among his many sheep, he took the poor man's only lamb instead.

When David heard that, he flew into a rage! "The man who did this deserves to die!" (12:5).

Nathan replied, "You are the man! . . . Why did you despise the word of the LORD by doing what is evil in his eyes?" (vv. 7, 9).

Like a hot knife through butter, Nathan's words pierced

David's heart. David's righteous indignation was replaced by godly sorrow. His anger was transformed into a genuinely repentant heart. David was caught dead to rights—and he knew it! For the first time in a long time, David saw himself as he really was: an adulterer, a liar . . . and a murderer!

In heartfelt confession, David said, "When I kept silent and refused to acknowledge my sin, my bones wasted away. I groaned all day. Night and day it was like this heaviness weighing down on me. My strength was sapped" (see Psalm 32:3, 4).

But when David finally confessed his sin—when he finally prayed, "Have mercy on me, O God" (Psalm 51:1)—his burden was lifted. His guilt was gone. His heart was made clean. And that's when Nathan said, "The LORD has taken away your sin. You are not going to die" (2 Samuel 12:13).

CONSEQUENCES OF BAD PARENTING

That doesn't mean David wouldn't face any consequences.

Consequence 1

"The sword will never depart from your house" (v. 10). Never again would David's family know even one day totally free from strife.

Consequence 2

"Out of your own household I am going to bring calamity upon you" (v. 11). Then he mentions just one such calamity: someone very close to David would have sex with some of his wives.

Consequence 3

Right on the heels of Nathan's "you're not gonna die" statement was this comment: "But because by doing this you have made the enemies of the LORD show utter contempt, the son born to you will die" (v. 14). And just as predicted, "the LORD struck the child that Uriah's wife had borne to David, and . . . the child died" (vv. 15, 18).

The Bible clearly teaches us that God is not mocked, that people reap what they sow (see Galatians 6:7). And even if you are forgiven—as David was—it doesn't mean there's not a price still to pay. And not just a price *you* pay either. The Bible teaches that even your kids will sometimes pay a price for your sin. Your compromise today can negatively impact your children's welfare tomorrow.

Tamar took her broken heart to her brother Absalom, the one who loved her with a healthy love.

That's why a child might be born with a drug addiction or AIDS. Of all adolescent drug addicts today, 70 percent of the females and 56 percent of the males were involved in some form of sexual abuse. About 95 percent of teenage prostitutes have been sexually abused. Teens with a history of sexual abuse are far more likely than their peers to engage in sexual behavior that puts them at risk for HIV infection.[1]

David sowed the wind, but his kids reaped his whirlwind. That's not to say that everything bad about this family was directly attributable to David's moral implosion; ultimately, every tub's gotta sit on its own bottom. David's adult children were equally culpable for their own sin. So not *all* of this heartache was David's fault. Sometimes a wayward child goes bad despite his parents' best efforts. But much of what happened in this family happened because David had created a family zoo in that palace.

I wish we had more insight into the psychological scarring David's sin caused his kids. But at the very least, those kids lost a great deal of respect for their dad ... just as any child would. Even more, they lost the consistent example of a godly husband and father.

They lost what should've been their faithful model for healthy familial relationships. Instead, those kids struggled for the rest of their lives with a family secret that led to a devastating cycle of other family secrets.

WIND DAMAGE

David sowed to the wind, and the resulting whirlwind included rape!

"In the course of time, Amnon son of David fell in love with Tamar, the beautiful sister of Absalom son of David" (2 Samuel 13:1).

Ewww! The dude fell in love with his half sister! And not a brotherly kind of love either. Can there be any doubt that this was a consequence of daddy's sin trickling down the pipeline? Amnon had watched daddy grab any woman he pleased ... so just like daddy, Amnon decided that it pleased him to have sex with his little sister.

He faked an illness and asked dad to send him some food via Tamar.

My question is, why didn't David just bring the food? This is his son, after all! Not only did David not even offer, he had no clue that Amnon's affections were perverse. This was a dad totally out of touch with his kids.

"When [Tamar] took [the food] to [Amnon] to eat, he grabbed her and said, 'Come to bed with me, my sister'" (v. 11). And even though she tried to resist, "since he was stronger than she, he raped her" (v. 14).

Tamar took her broken heart to her brother Absalom, the one who loved her with a healthy love. And he was furious with Amnon! (Absalom held a grudge, as we'll see).

How revealing that Tamar didn't tell dad! He was the

most powerful man in the kingdom and the one called by God to provide protection for his little girl, yet David was nowhere to be found.

Later, "when King David heard all this, he was furious" (v. 21). I wish the verse continued to say: "And in his rage, he disciplined Amnon by kicking him out of the palace!" But it doesn't say that. You know why? What's David gonna do— yell at Amnon for being a chip off the old block? Where do you think Amnon got his lusty sense of entitlement? How could David punish Junior for taking a page from his own playbook?

So David knew all about the rape but didn't do anything about it.

David had two opportunities to get involved. He could've delivered the food, thereby preventing the rape in the first place. He also could have prevented the murder because Absalom actually invited dad to join his brothers on what he called a sheep-shearing expedition (see v. 24), except David was too busy. He couldn't break away. He had king stuff to do. Yet it was on that very trip that Absalom got Amnon really, really drunk . . . and then killed him!

That sure resembles what dad had done with Uriah, doesn't it?

How did David respond? He tore his clothes, fell to the ground, and cried like a baby. But he didn't find Absalom and thank him for doing what David should've done; namely, exact revenge against his daughter's rapist! Instead, David gave Absalom the silent treatment. He was ticked.

Fearing his father's anger, Absalom went underground. And even though he was staying with his grandpa (see 2 Samuel 3:3; 13:37), we find no hint that David even tried to reach out to that young man. Instead, Absalom remained his father's fugitive for three years.

Finally, David couldn't take it anymore, so he sent one

of his lieutenants to bring Absalom home. I've got another question: how come David didn't go himself? He probably had an important dinner meeting or some client he needed to stroke, big important king that he was. But from where Absalom was sitting, the message was clear: *Dad didn't come because Dad doesn't care!*

For three years, David punished Absalom by giving him the silent treatment. Then he pulled a huge power play by sending somebody else (not even someone in the family) to come drag him home. And when Absalom returned, David sent him to his room. "The king said, 'He must go to his own house; he must not see my face'" (14:24).

Like many fathers, David behaved as though a thing hadn't happened if he chose not to remember that it happened. And since he didn't want to remember the part he could've played in Tamar's defense or the punishment he should've exacted on her behalf, David pretended that Absalom killed Amnon without cause!

The truth is, Absalom's rage was fundamentally the result of David's neglect! Yet "Absalom lived two years in Jerusalem without seeing the king's face" (v. 28).

During those years, both father and son bottled it all up. They did what men still do—shuttered their emotions and boarded up their hearts, both men suffering immeasurably from this self-imposed captivity. They spent two years on a slow boil, reheating every past wrong and every abusive instance with a smoldering grief and a simmering toxic anger that absolutely refused to burn out.

Those silent screams went unheard and unheeded until the powerful current of each man's rage slowly pulled them under.

Twice during this whole long story, we see David's feelings. The Bible says, "The king longed to go to Absalom" (13:39) and "The king's heart longed for Absalom" (14:1).

But David would not humble himself and go to Absalom. Talk about stupid male ego!

Payback

Can you imagine the impact on Absalom if David had actually gone to him and allowed him to see his tears? Absalom wanted it over too. He actually tried to make an opportunity to plead with his only conduit to dad, Lt. Joab. Absalom wanted to say, "I need to see Dad! Tell him I want to see him, OK?" (see 14:29). And when Joab refused, just to underscore Absalom's passionate desire to reconnect with his dad, Absalom set Joab's fields on fire!

Children still do that, by the way. When they're ignored by their parents for too long, they tend to start setting their *own* fields on fire. They will do practically anything to secure their parents' attention, even if it's negative attention! A teenage girl deliberately gets pregnant just so her parents will spend time with her. Other kids try alcohol or drugs or attempt suicide, desperately crying out for a relationship with distracted, even distanced, parents. Just like Absalom, they're left completely out of mom and dad's emotional loop. Oh, maybe they do get to see dad's face now and again, but it's usually in the blue reflection of a television.

Recent statistics reveal "that while teenagers watch an average of 21 hours of television per week, they spend only 35 minutes per week actually talking with their fathers."[2] Complicating matters is the fact that "one in four parents reports eating four or less meals a week together as a family" and 10 percent eat only one meal with their teens, if that.[3]

And instead of passing down values, encouraging good study habits, and nurturing affirming friendship choices in a positive, loving environment, most parents use the limited time they *do* invest in their kids to execute what I call drive-by parenting. They make mental notes of everything bad, stupid, and counterproductive their kids have been doing in the last week or so, and then during the five minutes they actually *do* speak to their kids, they pull out their parental Uzis and let them have it!

Even though positive affirmation is key to healthy child development, parents who take adequate time to say and show "I love you" are few and far between. Chats involving "Here's what I'm observing right now; let's talk about it" are often nonexistent. But there is nothing a child wants more from his parents than positive attention and loving affirmation.

That's what Absalom wanted . . . and needed. But not having such a relationship is exactly why Absalom's world was so messed up and why, like a cancer, his resentment of daddy's neglect kept building until it finally found a way to be fully expressed.

Absalom conceived a plan to overthrow his father's throne, and he almost pulled it off! He stood at the city gates and shook hands, kissed babies, and made all sorts of lavish campaign promises—all with one goal: Absalom was making daddy pay!

Absalom won the palace, he won the military, he won the hearts of the people . . . and as David fled for his life, Absalom pitched a tent on the palace roof and had sex with his daddy's women "in the sight of all Israel" (16:22).

Parents who take adequate time to say and show "I love you" are few and far between.

Isn't that amazing? Absalom violated his father's concubines in the very same place where daddy had lusted after Bathsheba. He was playing yet another page from his dad's playbook. Absalom, like it or not, was more like his dad than he cared to admit!

The only thing that stopped Absalom was a freak accident. As the mule he was riding went under an oak tree, Absalom's hair got caught in the tree. He was left hanging in midair, while the mule kept walking. Then David's Lt. Joab found Absalom and plunged three javelins into his heart (18:9-14).

TOO LITTLE TIME, TOO MANY TEARS

Maybe it was just my Sunday school teacher, but when I first learned about Absalom, I thought he was the bad guy. The truth is, all this destruction can be traced back to a lusty dad who got so caught up in his own desires that he left his kids dangerously exposed and alone. No wonder so many of them crashed and burned.

David was a great warrior, a powerful king, and absolutely adored by his subjects. But his children knew the sad truth about his parenting: daddy wasn't there when they needed him.

And that's why David was so distraught when he learned that Absalom was dead. Even though they hadn't spoken for many years, David "was shaken. He went up to the room over the gateway and wept. . . . 'O my son Absalom! My son, my son Absalom! If only I had died instead of you!'" (18:33).

David sat there weeping without consolation for the loss of a son, a son he never had time for. If only he had wept *with* his son. If only he had shown such unbridled love while Absalom was alive to see his father's passion! As it was, Absalom died never knowing how much his daddy truly loved him.

OUT OF SIGHT

In spite of David's many other impressive accomplishments, he was the classic absentee father. The man was practically never at home. In his mind, there were too many battles to fight, too many projects to complete, too many soldiers to

lead, too many decisions to make, and too many wives to please.

Still another of David's sons, Adonijah, also rebelled. And we're even told why: "His father had never interfered with him by asking, 'Why do you behave as you do?'" (1 Kings 1:6). In other words, David never got involved. He never crossed his son. He never said, "Put that down!" And he never did because he was never around.

Sadly, David's family tragedy is not unique. In one form or another, it occurs in the homes of businessmen, athletes, celebrities, medical professionals, sales reps, politicians, and even ministers.

- ◆ "I don't have time right now, son. Go out and play." *Someone else will pick up the slack. Mom, Granddad, a teacher, some youth pastor . . .*
- ◆ "What's that? Well, of course I love you!" *Why else would I buy you that BMW? And I'm sending you to a private school 'cause nothing is too good for my boy!* "But son, I've got a meeting. I've got this trip. I need to answer my e-mail."

And even though our kids need the affection and unhurried attention of their dads far more than they need an Ivy League education or an X-Box 360, far too many dads, like David, simply disappear into yet another cloud of dust.

OUT OF TOUCH

David had no clue what was going on in the lives of his boys. Had he spent some time with Amnon, maybe he would've observed his son's destructive and lustful bent. Had he taken some time to hang out with Absalom, maybe he could've diffused some of that misguided anger. But he didn't. He could have, but he didn't.

In twenty-first century America, it's almost inevitable that a vigorous competition exists between a man's job and his family. And finding that delicate balance is anything but easy. However, the stakes demand your constant vigilance.

It's not always a major investment that's required. Even more important than big, lavish events is your willingness, with some degree of regularity, to just stop what you're doing and listen. Do you realize that one of the big reasons teens stop talking to their parents is because their parents are almost always too busy to listen? But work can be finished later. Television can certainly wait. And the Internet will get along just fine without you.

Engage with your children; the very fact that you love them enough to give them your time will go a long way in developing in them a thirst for the things you hold most dear. And when you invest that time, listen more than you talk. Ears communicate love much better than lips do.

Find a hot button guaranteed to unleash your children's lips; then just sit back and listen. Sometimes you'll have to sit through some silence before they finally open up; but when they do, you'll strike gold. And what you'll discover will be worth every TV show you missed.

OUT OF LINE, OUT OF CONTROL

David's story should stand as a warning to us that kids suffer when parents get out of line. Even though kids may be angry about their parents' sins, they often imitate—and even magnify—the very patterns they hated most in their parents.

A young man we'll call Mark phoned my dad (a minister) and said, "Sir, would you pray with me? My mother and her boyfriend are almost home. When they walk through the door, I'm gonna blow them away with this loaded rifle. Then I'm gonna blow *me* away. Please pray for me."

Dad somehow persuaded Mark to let him go to his house to pray with him. When Dad walked in the door, the man was clutching a loaded and cocked 30.06 in his crippled hand. As they shook hands, Mark inadvertently dragged the gun's muzzle right across Dad's belt buckle.

In an extremely agitated state, Mark told his story, which included child abuse from his earliest memory. Mark's mother had lived with an endless series of boyfriends.

One time he was locked inside a travel trailer for several days. His mother and friend would stop by occasionally to throw some food on the floor; then when Mark reached for it, they'd kick it away and laugh.

David's story should stand as a warning to us that kids suffer when parents get out of line.

Now at age twenty-one, Mark had been treating his girlfriend like his mama had treated him. His mother actually reported him and was planning to commit him into psychiatric care. Confused and filled with rage, he vowed to kill them all.

Not all stories are that extreme. But dark and dreadful time bombs tick in the hearts of those who were distanced from their parents and disillusioned by their hypocrisy and sin.

David was out of sight, out of touch, and out of line. In short, he was out of control. That's why when Tamar was raped, David was furious but nothing more. And that's why, though his heart longed for Absalom, he stoically stuffed his feelings and hid behind closed doors.

What's a dad supposed to do when he realizes, *My boy is just like me?* Sex on the rooftop, alcohol-induced violence, deception and lies wreaking havoc on the entire household . . . David was so paralyzed by his guilt and his grief that he took one look at his son's playbook and mournfully realized, *That was* my *playbook too.* And he didn't do anything. Even though Absalom's actions resulted from David's *unintended* neglect, we must understand that the damage caused by a parent's out-of-control lifestyle is damage nonetheless.

Maybe you're successful at what you do, but all your success has bought for you is a great fear of trying to keep it going. So you get up even earlier and work even later than before. You go in on Saturdays and take work home for Sundays. Or maybe you sneak out of the house before anybody's awake—and then kiss 'em on the cheek at night because they're already fast asleep. Or maybe you sit alone in the kitchen, eating a nuked revision of dinner and telling yourself that you're doing this madness for your loved ones upstairs.

David may have blown it with his other sons, but at least he had chosen to do it right this time.

But you're so frazzled, you sometimes get in the car and five minutes later forget where you're going! You climb into an elevator and forget which button to push. You walk through a revolving door and can't remember whether you're coming or going.

Maybe like David you are really tapped out. Maybe you feel out of control.

Not Out of Time

But there's one thing you're not out of: time. David wasn't out of time either. Two sons were dead, but Solomon wasn't. And Solomon was God's chosen successor to David's throne.

It's true that David failed Amnon and Absalom and Adonijah—and he wasn't there when Tamar needed him either. But instead of grinding out the rest of his life in paralyzing guilt, David zeroed in on Solomon instead. And he flowed into that young man's life with a vengeance. He taught him the ways of God. He modeled before him a faithfulness and a purity that would, for the greater part of David's life, mark him as a man with an incredible heart for God.

As David neared his own death, he said to young Solomon: "Acknowledge the God of your father, and serve him with wholehearted devotion and with a willing mind, for the LORD searches every heart and understands every motive behind the thoughts. If you seek him, he will be found by you. . . . Be strong and do the work" (1 Chronicles 28:9, 10).

Wow! What a powerful legacy to leave your son! David may have blown it with his other sons, but at least he had chosen to do it right this time.

As I grew up, I never doubted that my dad loved me. But for some reason, he could never bring himself to actually say that he loved me. My dad was a card-carrying member of "the greatest generation." His father died during the Great Depression. And because there was no government assistance, my dad and his siblings had to scratch for every dime they could find—and every nickel went right into the family kitty.

As a teenager, my dad sang at war bond rallies, and the money he earned always went to pay bills. When he was seventeen, he lied about his age, enlisted in the Army, and served during World War II.

Dad was also a championship boxer. He had shoulders as wide as Texas and a huge barrel chest. I grew up convinced that my dad, were he so inclined, could "whup just about anybody," but I had especially intimate knowledge regarding his ability to whup me. Whenever I got into trouble, Mom said, "Wait till your father gets home!" I'd mope the rest of the day just watching the clock. And when Dad finally arrived, down to the basement we would go.

Years later when I was in college—and found myself trying to make all those pieces fit in my life puzzle—I'd call home (collect, of course) and end every conversation by saying, "I love you, Dad." I could just feel his strain over the phone.

Most times he could only stammer out a very tortured, "OK . . . see you, son."

I can still remember the time he first squeezed out a very frail, but equally genuine, "Me too."

Then as both my family and the church I served began to grow, phone calls would include his uncomfortable, but very welcome, "I'm proud of you, son."

"Thanks, Dad," I would say, and follow with the line: "I love you, Dad." These words were behind the most searching question of my life.

It was several years before it happened, but I can still remember the time he first squeezed out a very frail, but equally genuine, "Me too." Yet that still wasn't the answer I was hoping for. I needed to hear those words, just three monosyllabic words.

I called home three days before he died. We talked a bit, but not long because he was so sick. I closed that call the same way I'd closed every other call, still searching for what I hoped in my heart was true: "I love you, Dad."

"Uh, I . . . love you too."

As I cradled the phone, not knowing it would be the last time I'd hear my father's voice and that those would be the last three words he would speak to me, I cried. At long last he confirmed what I thought I knew, but really needed to hear. *My father loves me!*

The question I'd spent a lifetime asking—a question not unlike the one my daughter had asked me—was finally answered. And having heard those simple words, I happily marked my dad's tab Paid in Full.

◆ All those fishing trips we never took because he was so busy . . .

◆ The golf game he never taught me to play—and the wistful feeling I had every time I watched him stow his bag in the car, knowing there was no bag for me . . .

◆ The many ball games he never watched me play . . .

◆ And even the memory of those far too few one-on-one encounters—with far too many of them held in the musty confines of our basement with me on the other end of an angry, hostile response . . .

Those encounters—painful encounters that I perceived to be his severe disappointment in the man I was growing to be—had caused me to question his love. But in this, our final encounter, three simple words were spoken, words that I knew were the true reflection of his heart.

In that single encounter, every one of my disappointments, every one of my dad's admitted failures, every hastily spoken word, every impatient response, every human weakness . . . were fully and forever forgiven.

That history is the reason why I never end a conversation with my children, I never leave the house or even hang up the phone, I seldom even end an e-mail . . . without saying those three words that finally erased the divide between my dad and me: "I love you."

Though you may *think* it—especially you dads—unless you say it, your kids won't know it . . . after all.

GIVING "SWIRL" A WHIRL

Mark 3:21; Luke 4:28-30; John 7:1-5

➜ PEOPLE LIKE YOU

Sam was adopted at birth. He always struggled with identity and belonging; he just didn't know it. He never felt like he fit in his family. Because of this, he got into the wrong side of life and made some very bad choices. Then his parents got a divorce when he was sixteen. Split parents, Sam's playing and using the parents against one another, parents who talked bad about each other to Sam . . . it was all a mess. His story has a happy ending, but it took a very long time.

Whether a child is adopted, a member of a stepfamily, or is part of a family that has experienced divorce, the issues are more complicated than with a child from an intact family. There are mountains of research on adopted children and children of divorce. The simple conclusion is that, in general, these life experiences do not lead children to easier emotional and relational times. Children need their parents; that's the way God designed this whole family thing to work. That's also why we need God.

If you were asked to name the most famous stepfamily in history, you might blurt out, "The Brady Bunch!" But would you even think to mention Jesus' family? And yet it's true—Joseph was actually Jesus' stepfather, *not* his biological father.

Isn't it amazing that the Creator of the universe entrusted the raising of his only Son to a stepdad? And then he placed Jesus not in some pristine, nuclear family unit alongside Ward, June, Wally, and the Beav. No, he had Jesus born to a woman who became pregnant before she was officially married, and then he had him grow up among a whole tribe of half brothers and half sisters who didn't believe who he was.

In Matthew 13, a crowd from Jesus' hometown scorned Jesus, saying, "Isn't this the carpenter's son? Isn't his mother's name Mary, and aren't his brothers James, Joseph, Simon and Judas? Aren't all his sisters with us?" (vv. 55, 56).

As we continue our voyage through Small World, we're going to track Jesus and his stepfamily. But I need to warn you . . . it's not pretty. Truth is, the entire family—including Jesus—had to endure some really tough stuff. Just like *your* family.

However, the way I see it, Jesus turned out OK. You can stop laughing now. Has any truer statement ever been written? So how's that for a hope infusion . . . right out of the gate?

My Beef with Blending

The most common phrase used to describe today's stepfamily is the *blended family*. I don't like that description because most stepfamilies *don't* blend—and whenever somebody tries to *make* them blend, things get really ugly.

Imagine that I have a typical kitchen blender and I'm going to mix together a typical blended family unit. We'll start with dad, so let's put into our blender a bunch of steak and

STUCK IN A SMALL WORLD

172

potatoes ... with lots of gravy! Yum! Then let's add mom to the mix—and what mom doesn't like salad and Starbucks?

Now it's time to add in dad's two kids—a son, age eight (whose diet consists largely of juice boxes and malted milk balls), and a daughter, age five (who loves Gummi Bears and Ho-Hos).

Finally, let's add mom's three: an eleven-year-old daughter (who eats nothing but Mickey D french fries, pizza, and Diet Dew), a six-year-old son (who chows down hot dogs and chips with salsa), and a two-year-old (who eats dirt).

Got that unappetizing image of those ingredients firmly fixed in your mind? Great! Now ... push the blend button. How does our concoction look? Like a purplish brown, gooey, lumpy bunch of slop, right?

That's exactly my point. Try to force your family to blend, and somebody's gonna get creamed. And it just might be you! When you blend something, the ingredients inevitably meld into a nondescript substance comprised of what has become totally unrecognizable parts.

The past histories of family members get chopped and diced—and all their separate experiences and realities are pureed with blinding speed. Simultaneously, emotions are torn to pieces. *No one* makes it through this blending completely whole. Is that the way stepfamilies are supposed to work? Well ... many try, but those who do usually get crushed in the process.

A much better approach is what I call the SWIRL effect.

What could be better on a hot, sunny day than a waffle cone filled with swirling, delicious frozen yogurt? Sounds good, huh? So you stop by your favorite establishment, and what do you see? This place is so cool, and the machines are so quiet as they effortlessly mix their batch. You're almost mesmerized as you watch those tumblers lazily fulfilling their happy assignment.

So you place your order: "I want a chocolate and vanilla . . ." What? "swirl!" And when the lever is pulled, your tasty treat begins to slowly, almost tantalizingly, spill from the spout, joining together in such an easy, even playful, manner the one flavor with its companion.

Forget *blending* your family. Blending makes lots of noise and generates way too much heat.

Unlike at some ice cream stores, the chocolate and vanilla aren't viciously mashed together via cold, steel implements— nor are they randomly blended into an ill-defined, utterly unappealing brownish-purple color. No, the two flavors seem to make it up as they go! They don't even care which one lands where. They wrap around each other almost effortlessly and then, just for grins, combine forces to create the best part of the whole deal: the curly thing at the top!

And that's when you finally get to enjoy it. I always start with the vanilla . . . just to cleanse my palate. But then it's chocolate time—so I lick on the other side. And isn't it cool how the flavors remain distinct even though they both reside in the same cone? You can have a taste of this or a taste of that . . . and then if you're really daring, you can go for both tastes at the same time!

But as you approach the bottom of the cone, you look inside and notice something: these two flavors have melted together into a beautiful, swirling portrait of unity. Yeah, it takes time to get there, but once you get to the end of the road (or the Rocky Road, as the case may be), it's kinda hard to tell where one taste ends and the other taste begins.

Forget *blending* your family. Blending makes lots of noise and generates way too much heat. Swirling is much quieter and—if done right—actually kinda cool.

I'm a veteran when it comes to uniting two families, and I firmly believe that swirling is a much better approach than blending. I've worked on it so much, I've formed an acronym: SWIRL. Here is my carefully chilled recipe for how you can give the SWIRL a whirl!

S = SLOW DOWN

If you're seriously thinking about signing up for the blended family gig, before you dive in please slow down . . . and ask yourself some very serious questions.

That's what Joseph did. When he realized that a baby was growing inside Mary's belly, he shifted their wedding plans into neutral and carefully evaluated the wisdom of moving forward. Now they *did* get married, but Joseph wisely hit the pause button and took some time to think it through . . . beforehand.

This new journey, if you're not really careful, can soon look an awful lot like your old journey.

I do understand your sense of urgency. After all, you have experienced life's ultimate heartache—you lost the most intimate relationship in life. And the aftermath has been excruciatingly painful, hasn't it?

But now, thanks to your new him or her, your hormones have once more kicked into full gear! You've fallen in love again, and the dream of a normal—even happy—family life is starting to look possible. In fact, you couldn't be more thrilled because you get to start a new journey with your special someone.

But listen—this new journey, if you're not really careful, can soon look an awful lot like your old journey. Putting together a stepfamily is one of the most difficult tasks I know.

It involves combining two unique family styles, all kinds of different personalities, preferences, and perspectives—not to mention a host of alternative traditions, histories, and (we dare not forget) loyalties.

Yet most people make the decision to glue two families together with barely more than a, "Hey kids, we're thinking about gettin' hitched. You OK with that?" Then they march down the aisle . . . and head for Cancun! Eventually they've got to go home, usually to a house full of disgruntled and unrelated rugrats. And *that's* when they realize, *This is gonna be harder than we thought it'd be.*

For one thing, each spouse's dedication to his/her kids, which seemed so noble *before* the wedding, now seems like a threat. A teen living elsewhere when the parents got married decides *now* to live with them. Individual parenting styles are more different than each thought—and the resulting conflict from that difference rages almost daily.

So before you dive in, take lots and lots of time. Take time to emotionally recover from either the death of your spouse or the trauma of your divorce. You don't want to haul all those ugly wounds into your *new* relationship. And take time so that all the key players can get to know each other *before* they must live under the same roof. Once the wedding happens, your future life is no longer just about you and your spouse. It's about those kids too.

- ◆ Kids need time to learn how to act naturally around each other.
- ◆ Kids need time to get a feel for your new rules of family engagement.
- ◆ Kids need time to have a sense of where they fit in.

And to get there, they're going to need the time (and the freedom) to ask all their legitimate questions:

- ◆ "Do I have to call him Dad?"
- ◆ "Why do we have to live in *their* house?"

- ◆ "Do I still get my own room?"
- ◆ "How come she tells me what to do? She's not my mom!"

And the two of you need to ask your questions too:

- ◆ "How are we gonna do discipline?"
- ◆ "What are our rules about TV, Internet, and curfews?"
- ◆ "Who decides where we visit on which holiday?"
- ◆ "We open gifts on Christmas Eve."

"But *we* open gifts on Christmas morning!"

Such questions demand thoughtful answers. In most swirling families, too little time is spent honestly discussing the impending tsunami-like changes that are about to take place. And all too often, the euphoria involved in creating a new family unit naively overshadows the need to consider the inevitable pain that comes along with it.

I'm not saying that your kids should get a vote on whether your union even happens. I'm just suggesting that you slow it way down and take some time to tune in to what's going on inside your kids' brains. And then do the same thing with each other.

What often tears most at the fiber of a swirling family is not whether the husband and wife have adequate love for each other, but whether they have the wisdom to understand the crucial dynamics and the patience to teach everybody involved that this monumental change is a process, not just a one-time event.

W = WAIT FOR EVERYBODY ELSE TO CATCH UP

Slowing down is about your moves *prior* to the launch of this new family. Waiting relates to *after* your new tribe is in orbit—after the decision has been made and the rings have been exchanged and the move-in has already happened. That's when you need to relax. It's absolutely crucial that you patiently make sure that everybody's still coming along for the ride.

When Jesus was twelve years old, Mary and Joseph took the family on a trip to Jerusalem to celebrate Passover. But when the festivities were over, Jesus' parents headed home without him. Mary and Joseph didn't even bother to check on Jesus' whereabouts till they'd already been traveling for a whole day (Luke 2:42-49).

Can you imagine how that made Jesus feel? All alone in a strange city, yet his supposedly caring family didn't even realize he wasn't with them! *Home Alone 5!*

It's vital not to leave any children behind, as it were. Your kids may "hold their peace" at the wedding; but trust me, they're not even *close* to being thrilled about this new arrangement. And not because they want to be jerks either.

You divorced people probably don't want to hear this, but your remarriage was harder for your kids to accept than your divorce was. The trauma for them is much greater now because this marriage that you see as a second chance at a new dream, they see as the death of their old dream. To them this is another loss, primarily because every child of divorce secretly wants his biological parents to reconcile.

And yes, it *is* just a dream! But that dream will persist until the day you remarry. Then you expect them to instantly adjust to a new replacement parent—yet all they can see is ... another painful loss. Add to the mix that they now have to learn to get along with stepbrothers and stepsisters (who are *so* nerdy and they don't keep the bathroom clean and their friends are such dorks . . .), and they've inherited a new authority structure. Plus a different house.

Please, whatever you do, get a new house! You don't want to deal with the problems of one team enjoying home-court advantage over the other team. Instead, start with a space that's new for everybody!

In her book *Becoming a Stepfamily,* Patricia Papernow says it takes the average stepfamily seven years to integrate sufficiently so as to experience intimacy and authenticity in step relationships. Fast families may get there in four years, if the kids are young and the adults are extremely intentional. But slow families, she says, can take as long as nine or even more years.[1]

Your remarriage was harder for your kids to accept than your divorce was.

It takes time to adjust to new living conditions, new parenting styles, new rules, and new responsibilities; time to experience one another and develop trust, commitment, and a shared history; time to cultivate a sense of belonging and an identity as a new family unit.

None of that should be rushed just because you want everybody sporting a happy face! It takes years to SWIRL ... so back off.

Don't force intense one-on-one encounters between you and the stepkids until the kids are comfortable with that arrangement. Don't demand equal say when it comes to discipline. And while we're at it, don't expect little Skyler to call your new wife Mommy. If it happens, cool! But getting there takes time—and you need to be patient.

Of course it's easier for *you* than for the kids—you made the decision to get remarried. Your kids, however, now have to learn how to live with the decision you made. So first slow down, and then wait for them to catch up.

I = IT IS WHAT IT IS

Your stepfamily is *not* going to work like a typical nuclear family. You're in a whole different scene, and so many of the black-and-white realities in your first marriage will fade into assorted shades of gray in your second marriage. What used to be plain and simple suddenly becomes very complex and intricate. But if you're going to survive this thing—even more, if your new family ever hopes to flourish—you'll need to practice acceptance (it is what it is) plus a whole truckload of compromise.

One time Jesus' siblings grabbed him and forcibly tried to take him home because they were ashamed of him. Mark 3:21 says, "His family . . . went to take charge of him, for they said, 'He is out of his mind.'"

In Matthew 13 when the crowd was making fun of Jesus, Jesus' sisters are said to have been "with" the crowd (v. 56). Jesus' brothers and sisters may actually have been present at this moment. Or the crowd may simply have meant that they considered Jesus' siblings to be an accepted part of their group: "Hey, all Jesus' family lives here. And they're just normal, regular citizens—like us!" (And I picture the brothers and sisters going out of their way to *be* one of the crowd, acting as "normal" as possible in order not to be associated with Jesus.) By contrast, then, the crowd singled Jesus out: "Who does he think he is? What makes him so special? Where does he come off acting all magical?" (see vv. 54, 56).

Accept that this journey is hard and that it will never be perfect.

We can only hope that Jesus' brothers and sisters weren't part of the mob that tried to kill him because they believed him to be a blasphemer. Luke 4:29 says the crowd "got up, drove him out of the town, and took him to the brow of the hill . . . to throw him down the cliff." We *do* know that Jesus' siblings didn't grasp who he really was. John 7:5 sadly reports: "Even his own brothers did not believe in him."

And yet there's no hint that Jesus ever got sideways about that. Instead, Jesus accepted it. Of course it hurt, but it was what it was . . . and no, it wasn't pretty. Jesus lowered his expectations and accepted what his brothers and sisters were willing to be toward him, and refused to get sidetracked by what they *weren't* willing to be.

Your stepfamily may never have to face a challenge quite that severe, but you *will* face your share of obstacles. The number or size of those barriers is not a commentary from God that you shouldn't have gotten married in the first place. Once you say "I do," your original wisdom (or lack thereof) in creating this family is irrelevant. Stop looking for a reason to walk, and instead find a place of acceptance.

Abandon your silly dream of "happily ever after." That stuff only happens in fairy tales and Shrek movies. There's little hope your kids will ever absolutely adore their new stepparent. In fact, there's a fairly decent chance they may never get beyond mildly tolerating him or her! Give up thinking that the stepkids will ever cherish the time you choose to spend with them or that they'll hit their knees at night thanking God for their wonderful new family unit.

It will be very difficult to love someone else's children as much as you love your own. Oh, you can and will learn to love them, but it's a different kind of love. And you both need to be OK with that! Turn off the blender filled with the unrealistic expectation of your whole tribe ramping up to some exalted level of love . . . that the kids have absolutely no desire for.

SWIRLing takes time! Remember the purple goo—'cause if you keep pushing, that goo will be you!

I'm not saying that you should bury all conflict or that you should just let those huge, emotional walls remain firmly and forever in place. I'm encouraging you to accept that this journey is hard and that it will never be perfect. You also need to accept that this new family isn't what your kids were hoping for.

Get your expectations out in the open, be willing to compromise (early and often), and realize that it is what it is—but with every year that passes, it will get better.

R = Rein in the Jealousy

Turn down the heat, recognizing that love will not happen instantly between all family members. Jamming unrelated persons under the same roof and painting a new name on your mailbox doesn't mean that the whole family will instantly love and easily offer care for one another. In fact, the most realistic view is that love and care *may* develop in your kids. But then again, it may not.

So in the meantime, refuse to openly compare your kids. And whatever else you do, don't play favorites.

Can you imagine what it must've been like to grow up with Jesus as your older stepbrother? If you think sibling rivalry is a problem when the oldest child merely *thinks* he's perfect, consider what it would have been like if he really *was* perfect!

A few years ago, I came across this list of the "Top Ten Sayings of Biblical Mothers":

10. Samson! Get your hand out of that lion. You don't know where it's been!

9. David! I told you not to play in the house with that sling! Go practice your harp. We pay good money for those lessons!

8. Abraham! Stop wandering around the countryside and get home for supper!

7. Shadrach, Meshach and Abednego! I told you never to play with fire!

6. Cain! Get off your brother! You're going to kill him some day.

5. Noah! No, you can't keep them! I told you, don't bring home any more strays!

4. Gideon! Have you been hiding in that wine press again? Look at your clothes!

3. James and John! No more burping contests at the dinner table, please. People are going to call you the sons of thunder!

2. Judas! Have you been in my purse again?!

1. [The number one saying is about Jesus. But it's directed to his brothers.] Boys! Why can't you be more like your brother?[2]

Don't you think Mary went there? There were four other brothers in Jesus' stepfamily and who knows how many sisters; surely they got sick and tired of always hearing about "perfect Jesus"! He never got in trouble at Sabbath school, he never did anything wrong, he always did his chores, he never talked back, he always came when mama called—the first time . . .

Parents set the tone when it comes to jealousy. You need to acknowledge that although some of the kids in your home may be easier to love than others of those kids, if you want to rein in the jealousy between *them,* you need to rein it in first in *you.*

L = LEARN A DIFFERENT DEFINITION OF FAMILY

This is the final ingredient in my recipe for building a strong, healthy stepfamily.

Learning a different definition of *family* reflects what Jesus did. One time he was speaking to a large crowd when his family stopped by. This is the same stepfamily that tried to forcibly take him home, the same family that publicly declared his incompetence.

When Jesus' followers told him that his mother and

brothers were standing outside, "wanting to speak" to him (Matthew 12:47), you know what Jesus said? "Whoever does the will of my Father in heaven is my brother and sister and mother" (v. 50).

That comment is *not* dripping with sarcasm. And it's not a cheap shot either. It's just that Jesus understood the truth. He understood that even if you do slow down, even if you do wait for everybody to catch up, even if you do understand that it is what it is, and even if you do rein in the jealousy . . . sometimes you still have to write a new script.

When Jesus' brothers didn't understand who he was, he didn't try to force it. He simply recognized that he had another family, a spiritual family, who could provide for him what his physical family would not. And even though his earthly family thought he was crazy, his eternal family came right alongside him—to support him, affirm him, and love him.

If you're a Christian, you've got that same family waiting in the wings to support you, which means your Small World isn't nearly as small as you thought it was.

The apostle Paul says: "I kneel before the Father, from whom his whole family in heaven and on earth derives its name" (Ephesians 3:14, 15). The phrase *whole family* is a reference to the church. Because we share the same Father, we all bear his name. Everybody who is in Christ is in the *family*! Whether rich or poor, male or female, young or old, country music fan or lover of hip-hop—if God is your Father and if the seed of his grace is flowing through your frame, then the church where you worship and serve is more than just another gathering of otherwise disconnected people. You are family!

And whether you're a Presbydist or a Luthestolic or an Episcogelical—it doesn't matter. Hey, you can go to the First Four-Square Community Bapterian Pentegational

Multi-Millennial Synod Covenant Free Bible Church of Our Living Savior for all I care. And although it may take four buses to display your complete church name, if your Father is my Father, we're brothers.

Your Small World isn't nearly as small as you thought it was.

You want to talk blended family? Our Father God has been swirling his highly dysfunctional, wholly inconsistent brood into the same family unit—kicking and screaming—for more than two thousand years!

So maybe you need to broaden exactly how it is that you define *family*. Without a doubt, Jesus was the most capable man who ever walked the planet. If not even Jesus could force his family to blend with him, what makes you think you can force your family to blend with you?

When people line up to sign on for the privilege of swirling two families into one, the question really shouldn't be, "Are you willing to stick with her in sickness and in health, to love and to cherish until death do you part?" It really ought to be, "Do you think you're smarter than Jesus?"

Jesus paid a visit to his little half brother James just after the resurrection (1 Corinthians 15:7). Because of that visit, James received his big brother as the Lord and Savior of his life. Even more, little brother also followed his big brother into the ministry (see Galatians 1:19; 2:9). And then he wrote a book—a great little book about how to live an authentic Christian life. In that book he said that those who want to be in the Christian family need to live just like his big brother lived.

Laura, a woman in the church I serve, affirmed my SWIRLing theory, describing that putting two families together is all about how you do the mixing.

It's like making a great dessert. Once you gather the necessary ingredients, you have to mix them in just the right order. Sometimes even the speed is crucial. If you want your dessert to achieve just the right consistency, you have to slowly stroke the ingredients, adding a touch here and pinch there to ensure that everything turns out just right. In that same way, wise is the SWIRLing family that keeps a watch on how they do "the mix"—continually learning from what worked and what didn't. Blending seems to suggest finality. But SWIRLing means we're a mixture in process—and everybody in the family plays a role.

One of the reasons SWIRLing is so hard is that after all your coaching, consistent modeling, and faithful prayers, it's really up to your kids as to whether they get on board. And the older they are, the longer "boarding" is likely to take. Once they finally do get on board, you'll know that SWIRLing this family was anything but a miracle. In our case, it required more skill, wisdom, endurance, and patience than my new wife and I ever dreamed we had.

Putting together a family is hard work. And all that swirling, blending, mixing, and combining can make for a very exhausting journey. But there is a huge payoff for getting it right. The biggest payoff is eternity, when our heavenly Father will reward you for your faithfulness. But there's another payoff as well. I can't tell you *when* it'll happen, but I *can* tell you that if you SWIRL your new family, it will happen.

A few years ago, Josh called Cindy and me into his room and said, "I want you guys to hear this song."

I said, "What's it about?"

He said, "Just listen, Dad!"

When Josh turned on the CD player, it didn't take long for us to realize we were in the middle of a very significant moment.

I owe you (said I owe you)
They say the ones you take for granted
You miss the most
Woke up every mornin' to grits and toast
School clothes spread
At the foot of the bed
Anything that I needed was there
You'd get it prepared (yea) (you did it for me)

Then we came to the verse that said, "You raised me by choice and you didn't have to." Josh hit pause and said, "Cindy, that's you. I owe you."

The song continued: "Though we had our ups and downs it's all up now." That's when Josh said, "Dad, this next part is you."

Lord, heavenly Father
I praise your soul
Learned to love you for myself when I was eight years old
Before then I didn't know about your grace and mercy
I just knew my pops was preaching
While I played in the nursery
Then he taught me that you so loved us all
That you sent your only son to die on a cross

Can you imagine even a little of what we were feeling as the song finished up?

When I stop, look back think about my life
You gave me your love whether wrong or right

Ooo I owe you come on I owe you
When I was down and out
And all my friends was gone (I love you so much)
You stayed by my side never left me alone
(I love you so much, I love you so much)
Ooo I owe I owe you

I'd been waiting a long time to get some kind of payoff for trying to do our new family right. And when it finally happened . . . well, I'm so glad I never stopped believing! Please keep believing.

And one day . . . by God's grace *your* moment will also happen . . . after all.

SPECIAL NEEDS, SPECIAL TREASURE

1 Chronicles 4:9, 10

➥ PEOPLE LIKE YOU

Mark was a preteen, but he functioned like a four-year-old. People ask, "How can you do effective therapy with someone like that who has no hope of progressing?" Easy. You do therapy with a four-year-old and listen a lot. We did a considerable amount of play therapy; however, most of the effective work was helping the family. Mark didn't know any different and therefore wasn't affected as his family was. His family needed help to understand what to expect from him, to deal with larger outbursts, to connect with interactive services, and to deal on an emotional level with their losses.

Support for the family with special-needs children is crucial. Without it, they will eventually run out of energy. Enlisting the help of extended family, friends, and professional services is what will save their sanity.

The evening news was on, but I wasn't paying much attention; that is, until I saw the haunting image of a man first rocking back and forth, then leaping off a bridge near my home in an attempt to end his life.

At first I was angry, angry that the media so blatantly sensationalizes such tragic events. But then I was sad because I learned that this same man had just shot and killed his estranged wife and two daughters.

I was even more troubled the next day when I heard that a family in the church I served was connected to this tragedy—and had almost become a part of it.

When I discovered that one of the victims was a baby, one month shy of her second birthday, and then when I learned that this little girl had been born blind, I was a wreck. And I had a question. So at the funeral, I found my friend and, nodding in the direction of the little girl's tiny casket, I asked, "Mitch, did Shelley's disability have anything to do with this?"

He said, "It had everything to do with it. From the moment Shelley was born, this family was never the same."

My mind was instantly flooded with images of *my* family. My mom's sister (and my favorite aunt) was also born blind. Her name is Viola, but we've always called her Aunt Olie. And although Aunt Olie's mother was a strong, godly woman, Aunt Olie's father was mean; some say mentally disturbed. He wanted Aunt Olie put away. He despised her because she reminded him that he had fathered a less than perfect baby. So great was his revulsion that if he was walking across the room when Aunt Olie was playing on the floor, he'd just kick her out of the way and walk on.

When Aunt Olie's mom, my grandma, could take the abuse no more, she left him—shouldering the burden of raising three girls . . . alone . . . right in the middle of the Great Depression.

More troubling images of other family members entered my mind:

- My father, who died from complications due to juvenile diabetes.
- My mom, who has lived her life in excruciating and daily back pain.
- My younger sister, who is a double amputee.
- Cindy's dad, who was a victim of polio and had to use a cane to get around.
- And our son Drew who struggles with developmental delay—and was unable to speak until age six.

No wonder Shelley's story gripped my heart. My Small World journey has forever imbedded within me a very soft place for those who endure special weaknesses. Whether it's a congenital birth defect, the result of an accident, or scars caused by human cruelty—my heart is deeply moved by those so afflicted. I am painfully familiar with the world of special needs. I am fully aware of the enormous energy required for those so afflicted to accomplish even the simplest of tasks. My family has experienced the financial drain involved in medicating and treating special needs. And we've also had the feelings of inferiority and low self-esteem that those with "weakness" invariably have.

When you have a special need yourself . . . you're not like everybody else. You look different. You walk different. You may even talk different. And the difference doesn't feel so good, does it? It makes you feel like a misfit.

ONLY MISFITS FIT

From God's vantage point, only misfits truly fit in! It's astonishing but true: our God is absolutely captivated by those who are weak. He cannot resist, and he insists on greatly using only those who are humble enough and honest enough to admit that they actually have needs.

Those of us who have all our faculties—with no discernible frailties—tend to trust in our abilities. Of course we seek God, usually only after having exhausted our own resources. But the one who journeys through life saddled by weakness knows, *I cannot do this alone.* So without even the slightest whimper of protest, he acknowledges his need. Or she admits her dependency.

Do you realize that every Bible family we've met so far—every one of them—had somebody in the family with a weakness?

- ◆ Sarah, Abraham's wife, was unable to conceive.
- ◆ Isaac, Abraham's son, lost his eyesight during his later years.
- ◆ Jacob was crippled and walked with a limp.
- ◆ Moses had a speech inadequacy.
- ◆ Hannah battled infertility.
- ◆ David adopted a young man named Mephibosheth who was lame in both feet.

ACT ONE OF A TWO-VERSE LIFE

I want to introduce you to yet another struggling Small World family. Admittedly, it will be a brief introduction, because this family is given only two Bible verses with which to tell their story. To make matters worse, those two verses are located in one of the least read books of the Bible, in the middle of what we who were weaned on the *King James Version* used to call the begats.

It's a family tree, essentially, of the Hebrew people. Beginning with Adam (duh!) and continuing through each generation for the next several hundred years, all that is listed in the first nine chapters of 1 Chronicles is a bunch of names! Big, hairy names like Amminadab, Keturah, Zimran, Madmannah, and Hazzobebah. Hard to pronounce names like Meonothai, Arphaxad, Jehoiakim,

Haahashtari, and Oholibamah (you must pronounce that one the same way sportscaster Keith Jackson says . . . "the A-la-ba-ma Crimson Tide!").

Can you believe that Jabez's mama named him Pain!

Sometimes the names are given a brief commentary, but most often there's nothing at all. There are probably five hundred names in this list. And if you ever decide to plow through, it's borrrring! (Sorry, Lord.) Enough to make the stoutest Bible scholar whine. But because most of us never bother to read the list, we miss out on a special treasure. Right in the middle of all those weird names is a great little story about a family stuck in a Small World.

It's kind of like the Spirit of God is just chugging through the generations—whipping off names—when all of a sudden he says, "Time out! There's something about *this* clan you need to know. The son in this family was a very special person with a very special need and a very special request."

The fella's name . . . is Jabez. And in 1 Chronicles 4:9, the first of his two verses, we read, "Jabez was more honorable than his brothers. His mother had named him Jabez, saying, 'I gave birth to him in pain.'"

Some commentators say this is a play on words, that the word *Jabez* sounds like the word for *pain*. But others say that in the Hebrew language, *Jabez* literally means "pain," "intense anguish," or "extreme discomfort." Can you believe that Jabez's mama named him Pain!

We're not sure why. But you get the sense that maybe her pregnancy or even the delivery was somewhat traumatic. Maybe the kid was born breech. Or perhaps she was confined to her bed during the last trimester.

Maybe the timing of his birth put increased pressures

on an already struggling family, or the baby could have had health issues that exacted a heavy toll. Or . . . maybe Jabez was born with a special weakness.

In his book *The Other Great Depression*, comedian Richard Lewis describes the events surrounding his own birth:

> It all started two minutes after being yanked out of my mother's womb in unorthodox style through the not-yet-in-vogue C-section; taken by surprise, and ill prepared for all the commotion; without any opportunity to make up my own mind on the subject of whether I felt like coming out or not.
>
> From the first words I *thought* I heard—"It's a boy. [expletive deleted]."—I had the indelible impression that I had already let the world down. . . .
>
> To make my early outlook even more tortured, I took the heat for nearly killing dear old Mom. I mean, give me a break! It was purely unintentional! What was I supposed to do, stay put until it was safe to come out more traditionally?
>
> Hey! I'm no baby! I'll concede, yes it is true, my mother did go through hell having me, and okay, it nearly did her in. There I've said it again. I've said it a thousand times! So let me once again apologize.
>
> And yet, I never could express *enough* regret. Throughout my childhood, I was repeatedly reminded . . . that my mother was lucky to be alive. Sure they disguised this pronouncement as a cute family joke, but I knew that they really meant it: My umbilical cord symbolized a tether to my mother's hell.[1]

That's how Jabez must have felt. Some kids were Faith, Hope, Joy, and even Grace. This kid got labeled Pain!

Can you imagine hearing the words . . .

◆ "PAIN! Time for dinner!"

◆ "Pain? Did you do your homework?"

◆ "Don't be such a pain . . . Pain."

Maybe you identify with this kid. Maybe your birth was also a bother. Maybe raising you was a real handful. Maybe you had a special weakness—and your arrival brought anguish into your family's home and a sense of *stuckness* that you've forever had to own. Maybe somebody gave you a name:

◆ The Problem Child.

◆ The Neighborhood Nerd.

◆ Four Eyes.

◆ Or maybe even . . . Retard.

You were the kid with the braces . . . the kid who used crutches . . . the kid with that ugly birthmark. Or . . . maybe you *had* a kid like that. You desperately wanted a baby, but the baby you got has more needs than you can handle. And just the thought of a whole lifetime of caring for that child brings to your heart great pain.

The early part of Jabez's first verse says that he was "more honorable than his brothers." That word *honorable* means he was heavy. Not fat, just influential . . . a man of weight and reputation.

Isn't that amazing? By the end of his life, Jabez had accumulated more clout and more prestige than all his brothers who *weren't* named Pain. Something about Jabez changed from the sorrowful anguish of his early days to the affluence and success of his latter days. What happened that made the difference?

ACT TWO OF A TWO-VERSE LIFE

The answer is in the second of Jabez's two verses, which begins, "Jabez cried out to the God of Israel." Evidently, Jabez was a man of faith. And in faith . . . Mr. Pain prayed a prayer: "Oh, that you would bless me and enlarge my territory! Let your hand be with me, and keep me from harm so that I will be free from pain" (v. 10).

I'm talking about a supernatural, divine intervention—a favor from on high when God backs up the truck, drops the tailgate, and pours his blessing all over my life!

On the surface, that prayer sounds vanilla, doesn't it? Four simple requests . . . big deal! But just beneath the surface, I find four huge paradigm breakers that paved the way for some very miraculous things to happen in his life.

Paradigm breaker 1

Jabez's first request was: "That [God] would bless me."

The thought of this grammatical construction is, "God, really bless me!" I'm not talking about some innocuous, vague blessing that excuses me when I sneeze or that blesses both my food as well as the missionaries. I'm talking about a supernatural, divine intervention—a favor from on high when God backs up the truck, drops the tailgate, and pours his blessing all over my life! After the tragedy of Jabez's birth, the pervasive atmosphere of pain that followed him all his life, Jabez needed a break!

Seen in that light, this was quite a request! Unlike you and me, Jabez wasn't limiting his prayers to something he could get on his own anyway. He was asking God to do something that was absolutely and unquestionably *way* beyond his reach. And because Jabez left the details of this blessing entirely up to God—including how, when, where, and in what measure this blessing would come—he displayed before God such a radical relinquishment that God was free to do whatever God chose to do.

When you pray like that, when you sincerely seek God's unbridled blessing without any additional navigation on your part, your life will begin to display marvelous things. You are praying for what God already desires—namely, to bless you. So how can it be anything less than God at work doing awesome deeds in your life?

Paradigm breaker 2

Jabez continued, "Lord, I have a second request. I also want you to 'enlarge my territory!' I've lived too long beneath these stupid limitations. I'm tired of treading water. I'm tired of being known only by my weakness. All I've done all my life is just fill space. But God, I'm done with that. I want you to enlarge my significance! I want you to increase my influence! I want you to intensify your use of my life!"

Lest you think Jabez was being overly ambitious, please understand—there's nothing wrong with ambition. And there's nothing wrong with being wildly successful either. It's obvious from the context that Jabez intended to use whatever success he received for God's glory and for the expansion of God's kingdom.

And when God's glory is your objective . . . then pray!

◆ Pray that your business makes a whole boatload of money!

◆ Pray that your role as mom yields a harvest of kids prepared to turn this world on its ear!

◆ Pray that your every lifelong restriction (including hindering disabilities, negative parental imprints, and life-limiting labels) will no longer hold you captive but that you, with God's help, will break free to become everything God would have you be!

Jabez decided that he didn't want to live the rest of his life the same way he'd lived the first part of his life. So he said, "God, enlarge my view!"

Jabez wasn't looking for a quick fix. He never did say, "God, you gotta take this *pain* away!" (although he did ask God to protect him and keep him from future pain). Jabez just wanted to be used. He wanted to finally feel freed from the limitations he'd been told about and which had been callously pounded into his brain, as well as those he had freely absorbed on his own.

When Moses complained to God in Exodus 4 about not being eloquent of speech, God said, "Who do you think gave human beings their mouths? Who makes them deaf or mute? Who gives them sight or makes them blind? Is it not I, the Lord? Now go; I will help you speak" (see vv. 11, 12).

Our God assumes full responsibility for the changes and alterations that transpire inside every fetus. He is the genetic engineer who calls all the shots so that your child, and the special needs that mark your child, were not an accident.

You may never totally understand why God made your baby the way he made him, but rest assured he made him that way. And although I cannot explain it, I know it's true that God is often pleased to use a disability—something *we* consider a limitation—to bring great glory to himself.

If God is the one who initially defines your territory, can he not also expand that same territory? Jabez prayed, "Lord, I want you to do that . . . please! Do that . . . in me."

Paradigm breaker 3

Jabez continued his prayer by asking the Lord, "Let your hand be with me." I think the idea was: "If you decide to enlarge my territory, I'm gonna need more of you than ever! I'll need your guidance and your wisdom. God, as I embark on this grand, new adventure, I don't want to go it alone. I need you to go with me. I want to live my life beneath your guiding hand because this thing's too big for just me!"

The apostle Paul agreed: "It is not that . . . we can do anything of lasting value by ourselves. Our only power and success come from God" (2 Corinthians 3:5, *NLT*). But such power is *always* preceded by prayer. You could be living just one prayer away from awe-inspiring, Spirit-enabled exploits that would leave even the angels sucking air!

Paradigm breaker 4

Jabez's fourth request was essentially an extension of the third. He concluded by saying, "Keep me from harm." God's hand is not only a guiding presence; it is also a protective power. Jabez seemed to understand that when your life begins to transcend the ordinary, when your influence begins to extend beyond your original borders, you're invading the enemy's turf.

"[God,] keep me from harm so that I will be free from pain." He didn't want his new life to "Jabez" him as his past life had! He didn't want to live with that old name even one minute longer.

PRACTICAL LESSONS FROM A TWO-VERSE LIFE

Five words in 1 Chronicles 4:10 describe the rest of Jabez's life: "And God granted his request." In other words, God said yes. That's the only reason I see for why Jabez ended up "more honorable than his brothers." It's all because, and *only* because, God gave him what he asked for.

Can you identify with Jabez? Your past has known pain too, hasn't it? You've had your share of weakness.

And the problem is, if you're not careful you might just conclude that what *has* been will *forever* be! That means that the only place you could ever fill is a small place. An insignificant, unimportant space. There's nothing wrong with small places—if that's where God wants you to be. But what if God wants something more for you? What if you were to discover that God really wanted to send you twenty-seven unique and amazing blessings, but you received only one because you asked for only one? How would that make you feel?

Billy Graham got it right when he said, "Heaven is full of answers to prayers for which no one ever bothered to ask."[2] Sometimes we do everything but ask! We wring our hands, we toss in our sleep, we chew Mylanta . . . We whimper and whine, carp and complain, bellyache and blame—but we never get around to asking! We solicit others to pray, but seldom do we ask him ourselves, even though the Bible clearly says, "You do not have, because you do not ask God" (James 4:2).

So ask already! Jesus promised, "Ask and you will receive" (John 16:24). Trace that logic to its obvious and inescapable conclusion, and what Jesus is also saying is: "If you don't ask, you won't receive."

It's as simple as that. And I draw these three lessons from Jabez's two-verse life.

Incredible abilities often emerge from those with the fewest possibilities

Most people who struggle tend to believe that the past is but a prologue, that their life stories are merely a harbinger of more of the same still to come. But that's not the case at all.

After having lived nearly a decade hiding in caves, scrounging for food, and dodging the spears and arrows of his own people, David finally ascended to the throne. Looking back, he said, "The suffering you sent was good for me, for it taught me to pay attention to your principles" (Psalm 119:71, *NLT*). It's difficult to choke down, but David actually says, "It was good for me to endure that garbage."

Good? How can you say that, David?

"Because in my weakness, I learned to trust. When I was in a place so confining I couldn't do anything to change my story, I put my hope in the only one who could."

Like it or not, the Bible says that the way of the Lord "is in the whirlwind and the storm" (Nahum 1:3). It's in the stony places, the hard and crushing spaces, that God accomplishes his best work. It's in places of weakness that God takes whiners and turns them into winners. It's in the shadowy valley of death that God shines his hope-infusing light. And we don't have to like that to know it's true.

There is no rainbow without a storm, no blessing without a sacrifice, and no hope apart from despair. There is also no love without loss, no progress without trials, and no joy without a dash of Jabez.

At age seven, Aunt Olie was put on a train and sent to a school that would equip her to be self-sufficient. It was a good decision, but because her family was poor and transportation was limited, she seldom made it home for Christmas.

It's in the stony places, the hard and crushing spaces, that God accomplishes his best work.

She learned to handle money, do chores, and care for her personal hygiene. It was at school also that she learned to play the piano. Today she is an accomplished pianist, having played professionally in many venues. Although she can read Braille music, she does best playing by ear. She can hear a song one time, then sit at the piano and play it back flawlessly.

Aunt Olie attended Morgantown Business College, graduating with honors in a sighted school. Until her retirement, she was employed at West Virginia University as secretary to the dean. She could type sixty words per minute and even took dictation. Today she lives in her own apartment, does her own shopping, cooks her own meals, and travels widely. Since retirement Aunt Olie plays the piano for her friends at the senior center, singing loudly and smiling broadly.

In spite of the fact that her own father thought her life had no merit, she became more than just a contributing member of society. My Aunt Olie is an inspiration to everyone who knows her. Because of her sightless condition, the people in her world have seen an immeasurable and indescribable blessing. They see a courageous woman who would not just lie down or roll over. They watch a woman who would not become bitter, desolate, or cynical.

Instead, those who are privileged to know Aunt Olie have watched her embrace her suffering and make the determined choice to rewrite her weakness into a love song to Jesus. She is the clearest example I know of how God's strength shows up best in our weakness (2 Corinthians 12:9).

He can do the same thing through you. No matter your scar, weakness, or label.

Your name doesn't have to stay the same

Please don't miss what happened to Jabez. His given name was Pain. But his lasting legacy is "more honorable than his brothers." See what God did for that man? He changed his name!

Anthony Taylor obviously didn't like being Anthony Taylor. People didn't pay enough attention to him. He didn't turn any heads. He didn't have the cash to live the life he'd dreamed of. So he took a new identity.

The only problem was, when Anthony chose his new name, he overreached. He chose the name Tiger Woods! True story. He was subsequently found guilty of using Tiger's name and Social Security number to rent videos, apply for credit, and even buy a used Lexus![3]

That's one way to change your name. Not a great way. Jabez found a better way; he asked God to do it for him. And God did.

So . . . what's *your* name? Not your given name. What's the label that has been attached to your life, the tag that people (maybe even you) use when describing you to others?

Jabez's mama named him Pain, probably because she was so embittered toward God for chaining her to what she perceived as an inconvenience or disability that she actually allowed her view of her son to ruin their home. That's often what happens. A disabled child in the home can bring abrupt or constant changes to life. Some marriages can't handle the stress and are devastated after the arrival of a disabled child.

Maybe your name is Fatso. You feel your fellow travelers' disgust as you fold into the seat beside them. So you've decided, *My worth is forever determined by my girth.* Maybe you have a learning disability. You've grown so tired of the shame that you're practically a recluse—so that nobody, not even your family, can get close.

While it may be true that you are not responsible for the circumstance in which you find yourself, you *are* responsible for the way you respond to that circumstance. The choice is yours: you can let your need so dominate your life that it ruins your attitude, undermines your faith, undercuts your priorities, and eats away your hope—making life for you and everybody around you absolutely miserable. Or you can let God change your name!

You can decide that the shattered experiences of your life are not random. Rather, every event of your life is just another piece in God's larger puzzle.

I have no sense from this passage that God's positive response meant that Jabez was now completely free from pain. Neither do I believe that God is at all obligated to remove *you* from *your* pain. But I do know that God's heart is for you to see beyond your pain and to move forward in spite of it.

Your suffering must not be viewed as some prison to escape, much less another cross to bear. It is, instead, an opportunity presented to you by a loving God who wants you to fully embrace it.

The key to surviving your Small World filled with pain is ASK-ceptance

You humbly accept your weakness, your special need, your disability, your less-than-perfect you, and—instead of wrestling against it and growing bitter because of it—view it as a gift from the loving hand of your Father. That doesn't mean you don't ask for something more. In fact, go ahead and pull a Jabez! And don't just ask; ask for something really big!

I started pleading with God to bring some great blessing out of what had been an unspeakable heartache.

I remember the day I relinquished control over the outcome of my shattered life. How freeing it was to finally accept my circumstance for what it was. At the very same time, there was also growing within me a confident expectation that birthed a nagging persistence as I started pleading with God to bring some great blessing out of what had been an unspeakable heartache.

That's ASK-ceptance!

You finally come to that place where you stop wrestling with God for the *why* of your circumstance. You now realize, *God is too kind to ever needlessly hurt me. And he's so trustworthy that I'm confident in his promise to fully accomplish his purposes in my life—even through this tragic, mind-boggling, seemingly*

---

destructive, and yes, downright painful experience. And even though your circumstance is something you wouldn't wish on your worst enemy, you know in your heart that God has his reasons.

Yet in the same breath you're still asking him for something more. Like Jacob, you've boldly laid hold of God's heart and told him, "I will not let you go until you bless me" (Genesis 32:26). In case you don't remember that story . . . Jacob walked away from that scene with a limp, but because he asked, he also received God's blessing. And though he limped from that day on, he also smiled.

Our God made a promise a long time ago. He said, "Call upon me in the day of trouble; I will deliver you" (Psalm 50:15).

He will. But first . . . you gotta call.

I cannot promise you that your Small World will one day be free from all pain. But I *can* promise that when you relinquish your self-determined right to be whole, when you stop manipulating people and situations but, instead, accept this weakness and still keep praying for something more, that's when you release the Holy Spirit to do something monumentally supernatural in your life!

◆ ASK-ceptance is trusting God even though you cannot envision a positive outcome.
◆ ASK-ceptance forces you to view other people of weakness with a whole new level of compassion.
◆ ASK-ceptance melts your pride.
◆ ASK-ceptance reorders your carefully cultivated agenda—and will build within you the kind of resilient faith that will not be denied!

God calls us to learn to embrace suffering as a gift from his hand. He also desires that we take him at his word, stand confidently on the foundation of his faithfulness, and keep asking him for something really big!

Find your place of ASK-ceptance. Embrace your circumstance for the gift that it is, but don't stop asking for an even greater gift. And in the in-between time, find comfort in God and embrace his Word, which offers such amazing, life-enriching promises as:

- "I will never fail you. I will never forsake you" (Hebrews 13:5, *NLT*).
- "The LORD is a shelter for the oppressed, a refuge in times of trouble. Those who know your name trust in you, for you, O LORD, have never abandoned anyone who searches for you" (Psalm 9:9, 10, *NLT*).
- "The steps of the godly are directed by the LORD. He delights in every detail of their lives. Though they stumble, they will not fall, for the LORD holds them by the hand. Once I was young, and now I am old. Yet I have never seen the godly forsaken, nor seen their children begging for bread" (Psalm 37:23-25, *NLT*).
- "We are hard pressed on every side, but not crushed; perplexed, but not in despair; persecuted, but not abandoned; struck down, but not destroyed" (2 Corinthians 4:8, 9).

Choose one of those promises, stand firmly upon it, and then do exactly what Jabez did: accept your circumstance and ask for something more. Because God's promises never fail . . . after all.

NO ONE
COULD CONTROL
HIM

Mark 5:1-20

→ PEOPLE LIKE YOU

John was living a dead life. He often talked of feeling an emptiness in the middle of his chest. What John was talking about without knowing it was a "hole in his heart." He felt empty because the relationships in his life were out of priority and balance. Relationships with God, himself, his family, and his friends were nonexistent. And he described feeling an emptiness in all areas of life: work, family, social, and spiritual. All too often his response to that emptiness was to fill it up with temporary fixes.

John's family and friends reached out numerous times to help. But without his own core resolution, John repeatedly returned to his addictive ways—seemingly more committed to destroying his life each time. Each return added to his feelings of shame and guilt. Then more feelings of hopelessness only served to fuel his addictive thoughts and behaviors, which in turn led to depression and distorted thinking as well as self-destructive behaviors such as cutting and even suicidal thoughts.

John was an addict. He reasoned his use as a way to numb and escape the feelings of anger, pain, fear, and loneliness. No one had ever taught John how to deal with life's trials and tribulations, especially not his alcoholic father. What John really wanted was a place to belong, to feel loved, and to sense that he had some measure of a handle on life. Yet he often felt the opposite: no place to belong, unloved by others and himself, and in every way out of control.

Finally, John's core resolution began . . . with a relationship with God. He had been *blaming* God instead of *turning* to him.

Talk about stuck.

This young man was living in the dead parts of town . . . because *dead* is evidently how he felt. Or at least he *wished* he could feel dead. Sadly, it was his search for numbness that got him really stuck. Bottom line: the only time this young man didn't feel anything . . . was when he was using.

We don't know a lot about him, which is obviously the way he preferred it. Evidently he needed his space, but since housing costs were at a premium, he set up camp in, of all places, a cemetery. That was fine by him: *Because grave markers don't talk—either to me or about me—which means, I can be left the heck alone!*

Further complicating this story is that we know absolutely nothing about his family, although he obviously had one. We don't know whether his parents were shocked by his sudden departure, or relieved. And we're not certain whether *he* was the one who bolted or they finally had enough and kicked *him* to the curb.

The chaos in this home was exacting a heavy toll. For all we know, there may have been younger siblings or a spouse to consider—or an ever-growing financial strain caused by the constant upheaval he created. We just don't know.

The Bible tells us that this man had "an evil spirit" (Mark 5:2). Maybe his parents didn't realize that. (And maybe some parents today wonder if that's what's wrong with *their* kids!) I can imagine his parents said what a lot of moms and dads feel forced to say: "We love you. And this is the hardest thing we've ever done, but you are no longer welcome in our home. And if you don't make some changes, you're gonna ruin your life."

Sometimes our Small World problems are so personal and feel so monumental, we wonder, *Can anybody relate to what I'm going through? I don't mean to be arrogant, but my problem*

is way too complicated for simple platitudes. And even if I had someone to talk to, how could I ever find the words to describe what I'm feeling?

If Only My Need Had a Label

Have you ever had a problem you couldn't explain—even to yourself? How could you ever hope to tell somebody *else* about it? You needed something, but what was it exactly that you needed? You didn't know.

Your problem eventually gets so bad, it actually drives you away from other people.

If it were a problem with your company's computer network, you'd solve it. Or a sudden drop in this quarter's sales numbers? No fear—you would know what to do. But what if your problem were personal, your circumstance so convoluted that you could no longer just fake your way through? You would have no clue what to do.

What usually happens in such a case—and I think it happened in this biblical account—is that your problem eventually gets so bad, it actually drives you away from other people. The situation becomes so draining that it alienates you from others. It forces you onto a kind of deserted island where the only known inhabitant is you.

That's what unresolved problems do; they excommunicate you from everybody around you till, finally, you're all alone in a huge, protective bubble—isolated, desperate, and without hope.

That's this young man. (I've always pictured him young.) Whatever daily dilemmas stemmed from his demon possession, his problem was so knotty, it had also become absolutely overwhelming.

Was It Something from His Past?

The DNA of the man's family dysfunction was splattered all over this crime scene. The pile of evidence we have makes it clear: life was not working out so well for our young friend.

- ◆ He had a family but was no longer connected to his family.
- ◆ He once enjoyed a supportive community, but he was no longer a part of that community either.
- ◆ He once had a promising future, but his problems had grown so gnarly that his every dream seemed forever dashed.

Mark 5:3 says he was living "in the tombs." A living man existing in a dead place. Have you ever lived in a dead place? On the inside you're a zombie. But on the outside you still get up, get dressed, and get to work. And because you're still productive, still paying the bills, still showing up for soccer practice . . . nobody seems to notice, but the numbness in your heart proves it—you're in a dead place.

You paint on a toothy smile because you know others are watching, but deep inside you've got a secret: *I no longer feel . . . anything.* You become so disconnected from everybody that even those who *do* notice the change in you can't seem to reach out to you.

Cemeteries and Chains

The manifestation of evil spirits was common back in the day—primarily because God in the flesh was visiting our planet, and with his arrival came a counterattack from the evil one. The imposing presence of the enemy explains our young friend's enormous strength (and a lot of other things!).

"No one could bind him," verse 3 says. And I'm convinced

that infers more than just a physical binding. Mom and dad couldn't control him anymore, not in *any* sense of the word. Not even with a chain—not the chain of a threatened curfew . . . or another grounding . . . or a week without his cell phone. All that stuff was old news. "He had often been chained hand and foot, but he tore the chains apart and broke the irons on his feet" (v. 4).

Every family rule was broken, every restraining boundary crossed. His parents said, "This is as far as you go." Yet he'd go further. He simply *refused* to listen. He was gonna do whatever he wanted to do. And "no one was strong enough to subdue him" (v. 4). His behavior had grown so bizarre that people no longer wanted to be around him; there was no telling what he might do!

He lived among the tombs, and not because he had to; he *chose* to. He had a strange preoccupation with death. He loved dark things: dark clothing, dark hair, dark music. Perhaps he fantasized about death—corpses and spirits come back from the dead.

Yet even though his graveyard residence had gained for him all the freedom he'd always whined for—and even though the complete absence of parental involvement meant that he could pursue every path he wanted and make any choice he fancied—the great tragedy this kid finally discovered was that his stupid family wasn't the source of all his problems . . . after all!

Even with all that freedom he was miserable. He was sometimes thrown into wild, uncontrolled convulsions. "Night and day among the tombs and in the hills he would cry out" (v. 5). With a frenzied anguish, this scraggly bearded, mangy-looking, hollow-eyed madman screamed obscenities that could make even Marilyn Manson blush! And it was during those ear-splitting outbursts that he also "cut himself with stones" (v. 5).

CRYING AND CUTTING

Although Satan's goal is always to harm, we don't know exactly why the young man cut himself. The story's context does suggest some possibilities. Since he had either run away or been kicked out of his home, it's not too much of a stretch to conclude that things at home had become rather tense. And since self-inflicted violence (SIV) is an emotionally based syndrome, it's obvious this kid had endured some level of emotional trauma.

Cutting may have been the result of the torment the young man was experiencing from both literal and figurative demons.

Cutting is a significant problem among young people today. Girls tend to do it more than boys, but guys do it too. Many deliberately burn their skin with the end of a cigarette, a lighted match, or even heated paper clips. Others scrape themselves with knives, pencils, or their own fingernails until they bleed. It's strange, but many kids who cut can't seem to explain why cutting makes them feel better, though temporarily. But what they *can* say is that cutting is habit-forming . . . even addictive.

Have you ever wished that your life was a screenplay and that you could be the director of this film entitled *My Everyday Life*? You are the director, which means that whenever somebody starts telling a really boring story, you can just say, "And . . . cut!"

"But I didn't finish my story!"

"No, we got it. That's a wrap!"

Or for example, you come in after curfew and dad says, "Where have you been?"

"And . . . cut! All right, let's try it again. Except this time, you're happy to see me . . . you don't care what I was doing . . . and you're so glad I'm home, you fire up the microwave and make me some grub!"

You get into trouble at school, and the vice principal is writing you up; but you say, "And . . . cut!"

That would be soooo cool!

That's essentially what kids do when they physically cut themselves. Cutting is an attempt to gain a measure of power. Most kids cut because they have strong feelings they cannot seem to fully express. Maybe it's anger or shame or depression. Kids who cut sometimes complain that they don't fit in or that nobody understands them. Still others cut because they've lost someone they love or they just want to escape their own sense of emptiness.

Many kids who cut can't seem to explain why cutting makes them feel better, though temporarily.

Undiagnosed mental health issues are another trigger for cutting. For all we know, this young man was also suffering from bipolar disorder. In the text we pick up some possible clues. One minute he was fighting people . . . and absolutely nobody could control him. In the next frame he was leaning against a grave marker . . . crying like a baby! He was violent, then depressive . . . He was compulsively physical—strong enough to break chains. But blink, and suddenly he was uncontrollably emotional.

For some kids, the trigger is an eating disorder or some other obsessive-compulsive behavior. And many who cut are dabbling with drugs or abusing alcohol.

Bottom line: kids who cut are inflicting physical pain in order to ease a deeper, emotional pain. One teen explained it this way: "It's like my emotions were pouring outta my body along with my blood."

With incredibly high levels of distress flooding into their hearts—and precious few skills for coping with that influx—kids cut. It's a false assumption, but many believe that if they can transform their internal pain into something more external, and therefore treatable, maybe they can find some relief.

SIV is an extremely secretive behavior—(funny how many of Satan's schemes are!)—which is one reason our friend hid in the cemetery. But long before he moved to Tombstone, he'd already mastered the art of hiding his secret addiction. He probably wore long-sleeved robes to cover the scars and bruises . . . even on the hottest days. Or he shoved his ball cap way down over his forehead so no one could get a good look at his puffy and heavily blackened eyes.

Something was eating at this kid, something so destructive that it systematically pushed him away—not just from his family but from every potentially positive relationship. That's what happens when you have a dirty little secret that doesn't get fixed, a private angst you cannot resolve. In time, your secret will alienate you. Even when your family continues to live under the same roof, you live totally disconnected lives. And even though your family really *does* love you, they have no clue who you really are.

He Seemed Nice

Every time I hear about the latest random shooting incident, it's interesting to listen to those who describe the perpetrator. His neighbors typically say things like, "He kept to himself but seemed kind" and "Sorta quiet, but he was a good person as far as I knew."

But that's the problem—you *don't* know! The truth is, you don't even know your own children. Not really. So often we tell people what we think our children would never do. But we have no clue what our children will or will not do! Instead, we ought to say, "I hope she won't do that." But don't sign the house away on it—because you don't know!

Desperate people do desperate things; and the young man in Mark 5 was desperate. So desperate he chose to live in a dead place, a dry and dusty space. He was also an addict (whose drug of choice was sharp rocks).

An addiction is the inability to stop a repeated and compulsive use of a behavior or substance in spite of negative consequences. Most addictions follow a very predictable, three-phase process:

1. Addiction begins when said behavior or substance is used to find temporary relief from a terrible feeling. The key word is *temporary*. No matter the source of your addiction, the relief, pleasure, or numbness you feel when engaging in that activity is temporary. The troubles that triggered the behavior are still there; you've just masked them ... temporarily.

2. Addiction continues as the user becomes psychologically or physically dependent on that behavior or substance. After the relieving effects wear off and all those terrible feelings return, the desire to recapture that relief reinforces the destructive behavior.

3. Addiction persists . . . in spite of all the negative consequences. Most kids don't intend to permanently hurt themselves when they cut. And they don't usually mean to keep cutting once they start. Like any good addict, they believe they can manage their use. But just as you cannot calculate exactly when your alcohol consumption is no longer just a diversion, neither can you know exactly how deep to make your next cut without requiring stitches or even hospitalization. As a user is clueless regarding the potency and purity of his dope, so a cutter never knows whether that pair of scissors or even the sharp edge of the tab on his soda can is clean enough to avoid infection.

Cutting isn't an attempt at suicide; it's an attempt to release tension, to express anger, to numb out, to gain control, to experience pleasure . . . to feel better—but not to die.

Cutting, like most compulsive behaviors, can become habit forming and, in time, downright addictive. The more a person uses, the more he feels the *need* to use. The brain starts connecting that false sense of relief from bad feelings with the act of cutting, so it begins to *crave* this relief every time tensions start building. The behavior the person began in an effort to feel more in control ends up controlling him. Isn't that just like the enemy?

Mark doesn't say, but I wonder if the one who chained the man was the young man himself. Perhaps in his more lucid moments, his scars disgusted even him and he realized, *I don't want to keep doing this!* So he tried to restrain himself. Then he didn't want to be restrained anymore but craved relief, so he broke his own chains and used again.

A woman decides that while the pills *do* temporarily dull the pain, the price she pays for using is worse than the original pain, so she flushes them. Until the feelings return. Then it's, "Doc, my back is killing me! Can you give me something for the pain?" And the addictive cycle begins all over again.

No One Came

The most telling part of this story is that the entire community (including the young man's family) knew where he was, yet no one came to help him!

Someone in my Small World was sexually abused when she was a teen. But it wasn't until she was an adult—and a parent herself—that the truth came out. Obviously, she was extremely upset at her father for doing what he had done. But her mom received the brunt of her harshest attack since she "should've known but did nothing to stop him."

Sometimes people know something isn't right, but they never come to the rescue. They have their reasons:

◆ "I've been through too many disappointments with that kid already. So . . . to attempt yet another rescue is a supreme waste of my time!"

◆ "It's not really my business. He has a right to his privacy."

◆ "I wonder if . . . no, I'm probably just imagining things."

◆ "His behavior is all my fault. What have I created?"

The *Why won't somebody come?* question is a tragedy every addict must face. Because most addicts have only one real hope: *Somebody . . . anybody . . . please come and help me.* They have a recurring Prince Charming kind of dream, that if they drop enough handkerchiefs out of the window, somebody will eventually ride by on a white stallion, see the hankie, and climb through the castle window to rescue them.

The behavior the person began in an effort to feel more in control ends up controlling him.

But what happens when you send out the signal—when you cry and when you cut, when you even try to chain yourself . . . all the while living in the stench and squalor of a dead place—yet nobody comes? What do you do when the clanking of empty wine bottles in your recycling bin doesn't sound an alarm that anybody seems to hear? What do you do when you just exist in a numbed-out, hazy-headed funk— but nobody seems to notice? What do you do when you're still coherent enough to beg God to send somebody to help you—and nobody comes?

That's what it feels like to be stuck in a Small World.

DEALING WITH THE DEVIL

There are problems in life—and addiction is one such problem—that can bring even a strong man (like *this* man) to his knees! And there is a hellishness you can go through in addiction that is so overwhelming and so complicated and so destructive that you can't help but wonder, *Will I ever get out of this mess?*

Then when those who know what you're facing won't help you, what else can you do but decide, *I quit. I'm outta here!*

Trouble is, just getting out can't fill the empty space that started all this garbage in the first place! So . . . you start cutting again and crying again . . . fighting one minute, weeping the next. Or drinking till you're sick . . . and strung out every chance you get. You're stuck . . . you're numb . . . you're desperate . . . And now, having successfully driven away everybody who cares about you, you are also alone.

The dark side doesn't readily release any of its captives.

That's *this* young man. All alone and continuing to deal with old devils . . . and *the* devil. He was still weeping among the tombs and cutting himself with stones. And though he tried to chain himself from his own addiction, his resolve to change came around less and less often now—and even when it did still show up, it seldom stayed very long.

So in desperate loneliness he wondered, *Will I ever get to go home again? Or is this dead place my only place?*

HELP ON THE WAY

Meanwhile, out on the lake, another man was in a fishing boat headed toward the cemetery. The lake bordered the cemetery where our young friend lived and wrestled his demons. While our friend was drowning in a sea of trouble, crossing the lake was one who could calm raging seas.

Our brave hero had gotten some of his boys together and said, "Let us go over to the other side" (Mark 4:35). They obliged, even though they had no clue where he was taking them . . . much less why.

But the enemy knew. That's why, almost from the moment they started across, a storm broke out. "A furious squall came up," the Bible says, "and the waves broke over the boat, so that it was nearly swamped" (v. 37).

And that's also why, when it's this bad, hardly anyone—except Jesus—will dare come and help you. It's scary! When the demons of your addiction realize that help is on the way, they'll do exactly what these demons did: stir up the winds and feverishly churn the waves! The dark side doesn't readily release any of its captives.

Although angry storm clouds may cause *others* to turn back, Jesus not only wasn't intimidated—he slept through the whole thing! When his boatful of experienced fishermen couldn't take the pounding anymore, they "woke [Jesus] and said to him, 'Teacher don't you care if we drown?' He got up, rebuked the wind and said to the waves, 'Quiet! Be still!' Then the wind died down and it was completely calm" (vv. 38, 39).

Jesus turned to those same men and asked, "Why are you so afraid?" (v. 40).

When you're on a mission to rescue somebody, don't be shocked when a monsoon breaks out! Quite often a raging storm is just God's sign that something really cool is about to happen. It's so close, in fact, that if you'll stand strong against the wind and brace yourself to withstand the waves—if you'll just hang in there and keep rowing your boat in the direction of the person you seek to save—it won't be long before that somebody might finally be set free!

The same storm that engulfed the lake also crossed onto the shoreline. And standing guard just off the water's edge was a somber graveyard.

In a scary movie, when the scene is set in a cemetery, you

can count on two things: it will be dark . . . and it will almost always be raining. Our desperately addicted, extremely lonely friend was now getting soaked by a storm. It's not enough that he was cutting and crying. He was also now running for cover. Trouble is, in a cemetery there *isn't* much cover.

As the winds beat against his body and the cold rain seeped into his badly scarred flesh, this young man surely thought, *I can't catch a break! My life is in the toilet! I'm even worse off than these dead people all around. Like them, I feel like I'm dead . . . except I still* feel*! But I sure wish I didn't.*

The storm was so fierce that the experienced naval veterans crossing the lake feared they might not make it. How much more distressed was this frightened, lonely man? Have you ever been in such deep weeds that you wondered, *Will I even make it?* As soon as one storm grows calm, here comes another . . . and another . . .

Has it ever occurred to you that those storms keep coming simply because Jesus is riding the path of those storms to wherever you are? The wind is swirling and the waves are crashing because he has determined that today is your day of deliverance. Your much-anticipated breakthrough can often be found right in the path of an angry, raging storm!

While everybody else was pitching a fit and crouching in fear, Jesus was napping. In the very moment you fear you might drown, Jesus is preparing to say, "Quiet! Be still!" Have you ever experienced a time like that?

You've been living in a dead place. Maybe you're in debt and you doubt your finances will ever get fixed. Maybe you're drowning in despair. Or maybe you're addicted. And just when you can't imagine it getting any worse, the storm clouds form and here comes the rain!

So you just sit there cutting and crying—and now you're also shivering. Your nose is dripping as you huddle beneath a scrawny tree that not only affords precious little cover but also keeps bending against the wind. With *your* luck, it'll break . . . and fall right on top of you.

But hang on a second! Just as quickly as it blew in, this storm suddenly stops. And in that eerily quiet aftermath, though you're still dripping from the downpour, you sense a Presence. And as you open your eyes and look up . . . there he is! It's Jesus!

And that's when you get it: Jesus braved your storm because it's time. Time to loosen your chains . . . and set you forever free!

RUN TO JESUS

The first thing our friend did when he saw Jesus was amazing: "He ran and fell on his knees in front of him" (Mark 5:6). In other words, he worshiped.

He didn't go clean up first. He didn't shake off his demons and break free from his addiction and *then* go to Jesus. He ran *immediately* to Jesus. Even though he had all kinds of problems, none of his garbage would stop him from worshiping Jesus.

Has it ever occurred to you that those storms keep coming simply because Jesus is riding the path of those storms to wherever you are?

You can never live in a dead place so long that your residence would ever keep you from Jesus. You can't cut yourself enough, you can't drink enough, you can't medicate yourself enough to ever keep you from Jesus. You are why he crossed that lake in the first place.

I don't know what you're going through right now or how long your storm has been raging, but you need to hear this message: the wind and the rain are signs that Jesus is on his way and your deliverance is at hand. You may have been "tombing it" so long that you desperately struggle to believe that. Quit *trying* to believe. Instead, just get up from your hiding place and run to him!

That's what this man did. He ran . . . and Jesus did the rest.

Run . . . and Jesus will deliver you. But only he will do. Anything less than Jesus is mere diversion. So if you're hooked on something or you feel stuck in a Small World, an icy six-pack won't solve anything. Nor will a sharp blade or a handful of pills. Such diversions will only aggravate the situation and further complicate your ever-deepening problem. You don't need diversion—you need deliverance.

So run . . . run . . . RUN . . . to Jesus.

Post-Delivery Instructions

It's one thing to be delivered—and what a wonderful thing it is!—but it's another thing altogether to also be restored. Having delivered this young man, it was now time for Jesus to calm somebody else's raging storm.

Run . . . and Jesus will deliver you. But only he will do. Anything less than Jesus is mere diversion.

As Jesus prepared to leave, the young man "begged to go with [Jesus]" (v. 18). I get that. Once you've been in bondage to something, you don't trust yourself anymore. In fact, you're downright terrified that, left to your own devices, you'll just get trapped all over again.

Yet Jesus said no. He "did not let him, but said, 'Go home to your family'" (v. 19). While being delivered requires that you run to Jesus—and only him—to be *restored* you've got to reconnect with your Small World. God is not just about setting people free; he is also committed to restoring to

people everything they lost during their storm. And that's why Jesus pointed this man toward home.

Most addicts share a common feeling of helplessness and fear. In fear they shut down. They become so terrified by their own impending destruction that they do what therapists call dissociation. They separate and isolate themselves from everybody because facing their reality through the eyes of others is way too hard for them.

When they dissociate, they no longer express their feelings; and they no longer connect with people, because they don't trust people. They completely unplug.

How do you regulate your emotional responses if you don't allow people in your life to whom you have to respond? To fully recover you gotta go back to Small World. And you need to learn (all over again) how to manage your emotions (both good and bad) without feeling the need to get high.

For many in recovery that means you find a sponsor— and you learn to trust that your sponsor is going to be there for you. You also learn to trust that he or she will help you without shaming you or needlessly invading your space. It's in the safety of that kind of emotional relationship that you learn it's OK to express genuine and even tender feelings. It's in a healthy relationship that you find true acceptance; instead of suffering additional rejection, you experience relief and, as time passes, a new sense of self.

It was denying yourself that kind of relationship that got you using in the first place. Cutting (or whatever your "drug" of choice) became your friend; and instead of dealing appropriately with your emotions, you masked them.

Jesus was right (of course). Having finally been delivered, this young man now needed to return to Small World so he could get a jump start on his recovery.

The night I learned this powerful truth, I was sitting

alone in my driveway. I was rehearsing the nightmare that had become my life, a nightmare from which I had no hope of awakening. While the car was running, I remembered a young man in our church who had driven his speeding car into an oak tree. I remembered the paramedics telling his family that he had died instantly. And I wondered what it would be like if I did the same.

I even picked out the tree.

But God refused to let me go. Instead, he raced through that raging storm. And when I finally realized that he was, in fact, with me . . . I, like our young friend, ran straight to Jesus and fell at his feet.

That's when God gave me a Scripture that has calmed my heart on *many* a stormy night: "I will repay you for the years the locusts have eaten. . . . You will have plenty to eat, until you are full, and you will praise the name of the LORD your God, who has worked wonders for you; never again will [you] be shamed" (Joel 2:25, 26).

I was rehearsing the nightmare that had become my life, a nightmare from which I had no hope of awakening.

Part of that repayment happens when you decide to pack up and head back home to Small World. So do it! Head on home, because our God not only wants to repay you with a resupply of everything you think you have forever lost, he wants your family to watch you get it back.

When the young man's family and friends saw him again, he was hanging with Jesus—all duded up, drinking a nonfat latte, and looking like a million shekels! (see Mark 5:15). And they were amazed! Actually, the Scripture says they were frightened and begged Jesus to leave their region. They'd written the young man off. In their minds, he had no future and even less hope. Yet God both delivered him and then restored to him absolutely everything he thought he had forever lost.

God wants to do that same thing for you. And the only thing you need to do to find his all-empowering deliverance is run to him.

He's waiting for you . . . after all.

WHEN YOUR CHILD PACKS HIS BAGS

Luke 15:11-32

→ PEOPLE LIKE YOU

There are countless stories about people who got off on the wrong track in life and did not recover. They are, unfortunately, the statistics. The stories we don't hear enough of are the stories in which an individual, family, or marriage *does* recover. These are the success stories where setbacks turned into comebacks. They often include great pain, anguish, fear, guilt, and anger. The road can be long and difficult, but in the end it might all be worth it.

One of my former clients is going through a very difficult journey right now. Her parents are prepared for her actions to lead to her death. There is nothing they can do for her. They have bent over backwards in many ways to help her, but she just keeps making promises and breaking them. In agony, these parents are now watching their oldest child from a distance—helpless, but hoping for the best.

There are times when the best thing to do is nothing. God, however, can do anything. Sometimes we just have to call on him and then get out of his way.

Forget *mad* cow. This bovine was downright furious!

In February 2002, the citizens of Cincinnati, Ohio, were gripped by an extremely moooooo-ving story.[1] After having eluded her would-be captors for eleven days, the world's second most notorious fugitive, dubbed Moosama Bin Laden, was finally captured.

Although Bessie was largely portrayed as a rebel in this story, the truth is, she was really just scared.

That very athletic and determined cow, while on her way to slaughter, had somehow managed to jump a 6-foot gate and make good her escape. Then she successfully maintained her getaway, attracting so much national attention that the restaurant chain Chick-fil-A (that uses a cow in their ads to urge people to steer clear of red meat) offered a reward of one hundred chicken sandwiches to her captors. (That's one way to "beef up" sales!)

Meanwhile, Fifth/Third Bank offered our four-hooved fugitive a role in their new ad campaign. And even Cincinnati's mayor got into the act, promising an udderly (sorry) amazing offer: if she'd just turn herself in, he'd give this rambunctious little dogie a key to the city.

Finally, the authorities built a temporary corral in the park where she was roaming; then they brought in some live decoy cows, scattered some grain, hay, and—it wasn't even fair—sweet molasses. And sure enough, Bessie sauntered out into the open. That's when they shot her ... with tranquilizer darts, but they still shot her! When she woke up and realized she was behind bars, she threw a hissy fit! Can you blame her? She flared those nostrils and practically destroyed the trailer they had put her in.

This wasn't Bessie's first negative encounter with humans.

Some reports mentioned that she had also endured several pregnancy exams, which can't be pleasant experiences. She certainly had no love for being grabbed by people.

I guess not.

Although Bessie was largely portrayed as a rebel in this story, the truth is, she was really just scared. Cows are quite nervous by nature, especially around humans, whom they try to avoid. (Me too, come to think of it.)

But things did start looking up for our bovine buddy. She not only received clemency from her planned execution at the slaughterhouse, she also was adopted by former Cincinnati Reds owner Marge Schott.

In this, our final stopover in Small World, we're going to revisit the very familiar story about a kid in the Bible who did essentially the same thing Bessie did.

Evidently, this young man was tired of being corralled by his parents. And in his view, he had endured more than enough of their branding. So he jumped the family fence and made a run for it. We don't know a lot about his early years; but from the context, I don't get the sense that this was a gravely dysfunctional family—or that the kid had some major scar caused by past abuse or neglect.

He simply was ready to move on.

A TIME TO LEAVE

My daughter Andrea is married and an agent of change in the inner-city school where she serves. But there was a season in Andrea's life when I wondered if she'd ever reach adulthood.

Soon after her birth we were mistakenly told that Andrea was suffering from a rare, genetic disorder. Some time after that, she had a seizure that nearly claimed her life. She stopped breathing, and I tried to administer CPR. The paramedics finally arrived, and Andrea was rushed away into the night.

During those long, dark hours in the hospital, I watched as my almost lifeless baby was cared for by a medical team that was nearly frightening in its efficiency.

After we finally returned home, I clutched Andrea to my chest all night long. I was afraid to leave her. I couldn't and wouldn't leave her! Because she was my baby! As I sat there, anxiously responding to every breath she breathed, every sound she made, I made her a promise: "Honey, no matter what happens, I'm here. Your daddy will never leave you."

Little did I realize the time would come when Andrea would leave *me*.

It wasn't a sudden departure. And unlike Bessie, it had nothing to do with rebellion. It was simply time for Andrea to go to college. And I was confident that this season of change was right—primarily because Andrea couldn't wait to get this new adventure underway!

But in the days preceding her big move, I constantly pulled her aside and said things like, "Andrea, I thought of something I need to tell you . . ."

Or, "Hey, Anj! Don't forget to do this!"

Or, "Did I tell you . . . ?"

"Yeah, Dad. You told me! I'm gonna be OK, all right? Would you please lighten up?"

But I never could. All the way to Anderson University it was the same drill: "Andrea, I thought of something else . . ."

"Aw, Dad . . ."

If you're a parent, you understand. You spend eighteen years parenting a child; yet in those last moments before you release her, you wonder, *Did I teach her everything she needs to know? Oh God, please take good care of her!*

When it was time to say good-bye and drive away from my baby, I cried . . . like a baby! For weeks Andrea had teased me, saying, "Dad, you're gonna be a basket case when I leave." Knowing she was right, I had resolved *not* to cry in front of her because, despite her bravado, I knew that my tears would set hers flowing too. Yet crying was the only thing I could do. And not just in her dorm room. I cried for the next two hundred miles—all the way home.

It was really hard when my daughter left me, even though it was time. Time for her to stretch her wings and soar like an eagle. Time to expand her horizons and move out from beneath dad's shelter!

When it was time to say good-bye and drive away from my baby, I cried . . . like a baby!

It was time, but it still hurt. It still *does* hurt. We've had more than one kid fly out of the nest. In fact, just a few months ago, our older son also jumped the gate. It's been a really good move for Josh. But it's been really hard for me.

It almost feels like a kick in the teeth whenever the next generation starts flying solo. Even in the best of circumstances, our kids can't help but think, *I'm starting my own life now. And I'm gonna get my life entirely right (*inferred: *unlike you, Pops!).*

You know they *won't* get it all right; in fact, they'll screw up at several points along the way, just like you did. You don't want them to mess up; you want them to do better than you did—and in some ways they will. Life being what it is, though, you know they're not going to sail through nearly as cleanly as they think they will. But because you love them, you don't want to rob them of all that innocent ambition, so you hold your tongue and just absorb the hit.

STEERING GOD-GIVEN DESIRES

In the beginning God created us to be large and in charge! He said, "Let us make [human beings] in our image, in our likeness, and let them rule" (Genesis 1:26).

My son Josh's desire to have dominion and to be in control, to conquer, and yes, to even outdo his pops is a God-given desire! I came home from work once and found Josh dressed up in his Teenage Mutant Ninja Turtle costume and standing *on* the basketball goal in our driveway.

I said, "Josh! What are you doing?"

He sang at the top of his lungs: "Heroes in a half shell, turtle power!"

God deposited that conquering, dominating spirit inside every human.

Since it was God who put that dominance gene *in* my boy, why would I ever try to take it *out* of my boy? (Yes, I know it's that dominance gene that causes kids to buck our rules.)

God said, "Be fruitful and increase in number; fill the earth and subdue it. Rule over the fish . . . and the birds . . . and over every living creature" (v. 28).

The fact that your child wants to be adventurous, strike out on his own, and lay claim to his own turf is from God. So when your kid is constantly climbing on the furniture, when he tears his stuff apart (and your stuff too) just so he can see what makes it work . . . that's from God. And when he puts firecrackers in the toilet . . . well, that's probably *not* from God.

God deposited that conquering, dominating spirit inside every human. So instead of trying to corral your child, *steer* him in a direction that allows him to express that ambition in a way that doesn't, in the process, destroy your home!

If you spend your entire parental career trying to beat that desire to rule *out* of your kid—or if you try to medicate him so that his desire to *subdue* becomes *submit* instead—you're messing with God's plan for your child. A better plan is to redirect those energies and all that boundless, misdirected passion into a godly pursuit.

My parents understood this principle, and they had ample opportunity to apply it because I had a real propensity for breaking stuff. Not intentionally; things just "happened" that way.

For example, I started wearing eyeglasses in the fifth grade; and every month or so we'd have to go back to the eye doctor to replace a temple or a lens . . . or sometimes the entire frame! I was brutal on glasses.

Finally, one ingenious manufacturer built an unbreakable eyeglass frame. It was the most horrid pair of glasses you've ever seen—but unbreakable! Our eye doctor actually called my parents as soon as he got this new frame, obviously thinking that I was *the* perfect candidate to test whether this company's claims were true. In fact, while I was being fitted, he actually took the arm of the frame and bent it all the way back—and sure enough, it snapped right back into place!

We got those frames on Friday afternoon, and on Monday morning—a very cold, January Monday morning—I said to a group of my friends standing out in front of school, "Guess what! My new glasses are so cool, you can bend 'em all the way back and they won't break!" I took them off to prove it.

Evidently, the manufacturer never tested its product in subzero temperatures. To this day, I'm the only kid I know who actually broke *unbreakable* glasses!

Instead of breaking me because of it, my parents tried to redirect me. "Steve, if you break another pair of glasses, you're gonna have to replace them . . . which means you'll have to mow five yards to earn the money. Do whatever you want with those glasses. Just remember—the next pair is on you!"

LETTING GO IS A JUDGMENT CALL

There was a father in Luke 15 who had to learn to let go. Even though his son's desire to launch out on his own had come sooner than dad wanted it to come, the moment was here nonetheless—and he had to deal with it.

I'm not suggesting that parents have no say in that process. I'm just saying the decision of when to let your child go really is a judgment call. Most parents think this big release should come later than it probably should, while teenagers tend to think it should come sooner than it probably should.

This dad allowed his sons room to debate him, to respectfully challenge him, and to ask life's really hard questions.

I was an early bloomer. When I was ten years old, I decided it was time to live life *my* way. Mom and Dad still thought they were "the boss of me," but I disagreed. I announced to the family that I was running away. I wasn't planning to actually leave; I just figured a bold announcement like that might really shake 'em up and I'd get more say on things.

Instead, as soon as those words spilled out of my mouth, Dad leaped from his chair, grabbed a suitcase, and started helping me pack! He said, "You want these jeans, Steve?"

"Uh . . . yeah, I guess so."

"How about socks?"

And before I knew it, I was standing on the front porch holding a freshly packed suitcase! That's when I realized that I had just made two fatal mistakes:

First, I was still wearing my pajamas. In fact, I even remember the slippers I was wearing. They were my monster slippers—about four times the size of my feet. And ugly! They were painted with fake blood and scars . . .

My second fatal mistake was that I was running away in mid-December. It was cold—and my pajamas were drafty. But even more, exactly how stupid do you have to be to run away a week and a half before Christmas?

My dominance gene was a really strong gene, so I started stomping down the street anyway—until my slippers slipped and I fell headlong into an icy pile of slush. That's when I had an instant revelation: *Maybe I'm too young to subdue the earth!*

I Wanna Run My Own Life!

The young man Jesus tells us about in Luke 15 was much older than I was. So it was natural that, in his mind at least, his time had come. This younger of two brothers said to his father, "Give me my share of the estate" (v. 12). He wanted to get out of Dodge and run his own life!

Evidently, his dad had cultivated such an open relationship that their bond could withstand even a threatening conversation. And not only do you see it here but again later, when the older son also confronts his dad with a fairly explosive response. This dad allowed his sons room to debate him, to respectfully challenge him, and to ask life's really hard questions.

There was no forbidden topic in this home—and no sulking silence to punish those trespassers who dared breach dad's invisible line. Had this dad not been so inclined, our young friend probably would've just run away. Instead, he had the freedom to honestly express his feelings. And even though we're not privy to everything he said, no doubt he was spouting off about "getting the chance to live my own life" and "no longer being tied to Daddy's rules."

But instead of moody silence, this dad heard him out, and then "he divided his property between them" (v. 12). No final "Before you run away . . ." lecture. He simply divided his property, please note, between them.

Evidently dad not only graciously cut his younger son loose, he cut financial ties with his older son as well. He divvied his property according to Jewish law—he gave the older son two-thirds of his assets and the younger son one-third. And he did it because this dad realized it was time.

"Not long after that, the younger son got together all he had" and "set off for a distant country" (v. 13). Life on the farm was too slow for his tastes. So with his pockets now bulging with all that inheritance money, Junior set out in search of the good life!

Instead, he found hangovers, fair-weather friends, and long unemployment lines.

Verse 13 ends with this sad postscript: "[He] . . . squandered his wealth in wild living." *Squandered* pretty much covers it. *The Message* says "wasted." These weren't noble pursuits our friend was following.

We don't know how long he was gone, but since the famine mentioned in verse 14 had affected the entire economy, and since his own resources had been so depleted that he was now also in need, it's safe to say he'd been gone for at least several months.

MEANWHILE, BACK AT THE RANCH . . .

What was dad doing all this time? Calling in Amber Alerts with the Jerusalem DPS? Crying himself to sleep at night?

There's no hint of any of that. Dad had done right by that boy—and he knew it. He wasn't perfect, but he had been faithful. He lived in a calm, confident trust that God would complete the job he couldn't finish himself; namely, change his son's life's direction.

Meanwhile, back in the far country, our young hero was getting fed up. He had become so destitute that he took a job slopping pigs (not exactly a kosher career move for a young Jew). Even more, he started eating the same slop he was supposed to be serving them! He "became so hungry that even the pods he was feeding the pigs looked good to him" (v. 16, *NLT*).

That's when he finally found bottom. He "came to his senses" and said to himself, "My father's hired men have food to spare, and here I am starving to death! I will . . . go back to my father" (vv. 17, 18).

Note that. He didn't say, "I'm going back to the farm!" or "I can't wait to sleep in my own bed!" He said, "I need to see Dad!"

No matter what you physically give your children or how lavishly you may provide for them, the most significant thing in your home is you! When your prodigal is dangling from the end of his own rope, when he's had as much of the pig's life as he can stand, he's not reminiscing about the size of his bedroom or his impressive PlayStation gear—he's missing you.

The prodigal put together a plan, including a carefully crafted speech that he rehearsed all the way home: "Father, I have sinned against heaven and against you. I am no longer worthy to be called your son; make me like one of your hired men" (vv. 18, 19). He wasn't going to ask for his room back. He would sleep in the bunkhouse if his dad would let him.

"So he got up and went to his father" (v. 20).

Meanwhile, back at the ranch, just because dad was trusting God doesn't mean he was twiddling his thumbs. I'm convinced that every morning this father was on his knees, passionately praying for his boy. I picture him leaning against the front gate with a cup of coffee warming his hands, just gazing across the horizon and hoping against hope, *Maybe one of these days, I'll see my boy heading this way.*

Mikhail Baryshnikov portrays that scene with an amazing passion. In a Russian ballet called *Prodigal Son,* the father, opulently attired, stands on one side of the stage with his arms stoically outstretched.

Then the spotlight shifts to a bedraggled figure on the other side of the stage. It's Baryshnikov, as the destitute prodigal. He's so famished he can't even walk. In a tortuous crawl, he wearily crosses the stage toward his waiting father. Inching along with a painstaking determination, he finally takes hold of his father's ankles. The father is unmoved. The son, with tears of repentance streaming down his face, slowly pulls himself up to his father's knees.

And then, in an amazingly athletic move, Baryshnikov lifts himself up into the air, landing ever so softly right in the father's outstretched arms. The audience first weeps and then cheers as the father cradles his boy in his arms. Even so, the father's arms barely change position. And had the son not leaped at the precise angle—exerting all the effort himself— he would have fallen.

Now that's very powerful drama—but it's not how Jesus described it. He pictured a dad so broken, you just know that he really wanted to chase after that kid and drag him home if necessary! But though he may have been tempted, he never did go. Instead, he patiently waited for his son to start his return home. He had released him—he willingly let him go—then he trusted God for his safe return.

If you're a dad who has adopted some tough-guy routine with your older kids, it's time to lose it.

This father was wise enough to realize that a rebel's heart has to get broken before home is where he wants to be. So he waited. Much of the time he was praying. At other times he leaned against the gate—leaning, looking, and longing.

No Before-Dinner Speech
Finally, the moment the father had been dreaming of arrived: "While [his son] was still a long way off, his father saw him" (v. 20).

"It's him! That's my boy!"

Verse 20 says the father was "filled with compassion" and "ran to his son." He didn't stand there, arms folded in disgust; he raced to where his boy was. And instead of demanding an explanation or verbally accosting him with all sorts of sarcastic put-downs, he "threw his arms around him and kissed him" (v. 20). In fact, the way this phrase is constructed, it suggests that he kissed him repeatedly!

That kid had been in a pigsty, and he absolutely reeked! He was filthy, downright mangy. But never mind that—this was a beloved son. And that's why his father immediately unzipped his heart and loved on that kid.

If you're a dad who has adopted some tough-guy routine with your older kids, it's time to lose it. Instead, make sure your kids know how deeply you feel about them. They long for your embrace. They never outgrow the need to hear you say "I love you."

To his credit, the son tried to give his speech: "Father, I have sinned against heaven and against you. I am no longer worthy to be called your son" (v. 21).

But the boy's words of apology were effectively silenced by dad's words of forgiveness. Forget wagging fingers and clenched fists. Never mind any of that "Where have you been?" garbage. All this dad cared about was that "this son of mine was dead and is alive again; he was lost and is found" (v. 24). "So . . . let's have us a partyyyyyy!"

BAGGAGE THAT NEEDS UNPACKING

Meanwhile, the older son was still "in the field" (v. 25). That pretty much tells all you need to know about him. In this family, he was the responsible kid. Little brother never could be counted on, but big bro always came through. He never did anything wrong, never skipped curfew, never talked back . . . He was the good kid. If you don't believe me, just ask *him*! He was the hard-working, ever-faithful, always-loyal son.

Trouble is, it was that self-perceived identity that had become his baggage. His self-appraisal was actually false. He really wasn't that good. He just looked good by comparison and, therefore, began acting out the "good" role.

Since his little brother was also his polar opposite, you can bet small fry had baggage too. While the little brother still lived at home, he probably got most of dad's attention (as the youngest child tends to do). Once small fry took off, big brother really enjoyed basking solo in dad's spotlight. Finally, the good kid was getting some airtime! He (and he alone) was now the unquestioned glory of this shrinking family because he was the one who stayed home.

CHECKING OR CHOKING ON BAGGAGE

The older son was comfortable at home, but he was doomed to live forever constrained by his baggage.

The "good" son, truth be told, may have wanted to leave just as much as his kid brother did, but he never could because his baggage consisted of playing the role of the *better* brother. He stayed home not because he was responsible but because his assigned family role was to be responsible. And don't think he didn't stew about it!

In 1 Samuel 10, God had instructed his prophet Samuel to anoint Saul as Israel's first king. But young Saul was a humble man and felt so undeserving of this noble assignment that when it came time to introduce him to the masses, Saul actually hid from his handlers. Having hunted everywhere, the people asked the Lord, who told them, "[Saul] has hidden himself among the baggage" (v. 22).

That's what the older of these two sons did as well. He hid behind his baggage. He never did deal with his own need to rule and subdue, to conquer and have dominion, to take charge of his own life and destiny. Instead, he resented his little brother for having the courage he didn't have.

That's why, "when he came near the house, he heard music and dancing [*something that hadn't been heard since party boy ran away*]. So he called one of the servants and asked him what was going on" (Luke 15:25, 26).

"'Your brother has come,' [the servant] replied, 'and your father has killed the fattened calf because he has him back safe and sound'" (v. 27).

This was the older son's *second* opportunity to unpack his baggage, another defining moment when he could've stepped away from an identity that really wasn't working for him. But he couldn't bring himself to do it. Evidently, older brother kinda *liked* lugging around extra baggage.

When I fly and can do so without checking my bags, I'll do it every single time. I hate wading through the congestion at those crowded carousels. When my flight is over, I'm ready to be home. I don't want to stand around some silly airport picking through Samsonites.

But the rules are strict when it comes to carry-on baggage. Now even lipstick and face wash are strictly forbidden (not that *I* need those!). Carry-on luggage also has to be a certain size. If it's much bigger than a grocery bag, "You'll have to check that bag, sir." If it doesn't fit in the overhead compartment, it's not safe. That loose baggage will rattle around and hurt somebody—maybe even you.

Perhaps you're carrying emotional baggage filled with things that people wrongly assigned to you in years gone by. You shoulder distortions, lies, blame, and a whole duffle bag full of shame—and all that mess is weighing you down. If your baggage is larger than you can easily handle, listen to your flight attendant: "Check your baggage!"

Isn't it time to forever unpack all that baggage? Isn't it time to reclaim your God-given identity? That's what big brother needed to do. But instead, he "became angry and refused to go [to the party]" (v. 28).

His father "went out and pleaded with him" (v. 28). He wasn't thrilled by his son's angry display, but he seemed to understand. Even more, just as with his number two son, dad allowed him to vent without getting in trouble for it.

The first word out of the older son's mouth was "Look!" And it was directed at his father. If I had ever said "Look!" like that to my dad, I might not have survived to write this. "Look! All these years I've been slaving for you and never disobeyed your orders [*like that jerk brother of mine*]" (v. 29).

Part of his baggage was, "[*I like it with little bro gone! He was a troublemaker, but I'm your good son, remember, Daddy?*] Yet you never gave me even a young goat so I could celebrate with my friends. But when this son of yours"—he can't even bring himself to say 'my brother'—"who has squandered your property with prostitutes . . ." (vv. 29, 30).

How did he know *that*? Perhaps that's what *he* would've done had he been the one to leave. On the outside, he was the perfect child, the model son. Yet when confronted by his father's joy at the return of his little brother, a dark and pervasive evil absolutely erupted from within!

COMING HOME TO YOUR BROTHER

I think the most difficult part about coming home isn't facing your father—it's having to face your brother. That's why many wandering prodigals never do return. It's not because *God*, their shepherd, won't forgive them; it's because the other *sheep* refuse to forget.

And whether it's a rebellious son or a frightened cow wandering away, we who remain on the inside can be so hard on the fugitive, primarily because we'll do *anything* to deny the darkness in our own hearts.

In Cincinnati, Bessie was on the lam because she didn't

want to be somebody's next quarter pounder. In Luke 15, the younger son waited to come home until he had no other options—for the very same reason. He didn't want to be judged or mercilessly ground into hamburger. He didn't relish the thought of his older brother's renewed slander or hurtful gossip. He couldn't imagine enduring another round of cruel stares and ugly glares. That's one reason he ran in the first place—and why many Small World inhabitants are still running.

When confronted by his father's joy at the return of his little brother, a dark and pervasive evil absolutely erupted from within!

But unlike Bessie's captors—and unlike the prodigal's brother—our heavenly Father isn't frowning. And he's not sternly waiting for his straying kids to crawl back from the squalor of our sorry lives either. He doesn't hold us at arm's length. He doesn't demand an adequate explanation plus a convincing apology.

No, our Father waits just long enough to see in us the slightest inclination that we want to come home. And once he sees that we are, in fact, willing . . . our Father, just like *this* father, races to wherever we are!

He doesn't give a rip about well-rehearsed speeches. Neither is he repelled by the stench of our messy compromise. All he wants is to hold us and lavish us with his grace so that we can complete the final leg of our journey by coming home and unpacking our baggage.

It's ironic that the younger son found freedom by temporarily leaving his Small World, while the older brother remained stuck because he stayed there.

And I think dad knew he was stuck. That's why, instead of arguing with him or reminding him that there had been plenty of times when he had disobeyed and many more times when his behavior was also far less than stellar . . . instead of debating with him, dad affirmed him.

"'My son,' the father said, 'you are always with me, and everything I have is yours. [*None of that has changed.*] But we had to celebrate and be glad, because this brother of yours was dead and is alive again; he was lost and is found'" (vv. 31, 32).

It has always fascinated me that Jesus never tells us how this story ends.

A familiar stopover for many Small World travelers is being stuck at the baggage carousel.

This poor dad finally got plucked out of one Small World experience only to get slammed right into the middle of another. And who knows but that the second was even more painful than the first! As the curtain falls on this troubled family, we have no word on whether either of these men ever made it to the family banquet.

Instead—as happens in far too many homes—part of the family was inside, singing a song of sweet restoration, while an entirely different tune was being sung on the outside: a dissonant tune filled with heartache and resentment.

And then there's dad. He loved *both* tribes, so he tried to hum both melodies—finding himself stuck (once again) between the banquet and the baggage.

Is that where you live too?

A familiar stopover for many Small World travelers is being stuck at the baggage carousel. Everybody's got baggage. Maybe, like Junior, you've got some baggage that needs unpacking. Or maybe, like big brother, you've got some bags that got packed many years ago, but you've been carrying them around for years, having no idea where you could ever hope to check them.

Jesus has a place where you can check those heavy items. Take them to your heavenly Father because, no matter the story, he'll be glad to lighten your burden. Like the father in Luke 15, our heavenly Father will help you lug around your baggage and then help you unpack it.

Whether you've always stayed around and been ticked because of it, or whether you were once lost and now are found . . . either way, just like the dad in this story, your heavenly Father's response is: let's throw a party and celebrate . . . after all!

EPILOGUE

As we come to the end of our Small World voyage, I'm wondering which family scenario most resembles yours. Maybe you live in a home in mid-SWIRL. Or maybe you're paying the tab for a dad who wasn't there for you.

Or . . . perhaps your family is like the family in Luke 15; your whole clan is stuck between competing melodies. Some members are still hiding behind their baggage while others are freely enjoying the banquet with little regard for those who no longer have a place at the table.

Doing family is a lot like a ride at Disneyland—you don't get to pick who rides in your boat. Your family is what it is. But please remember the following two truths . . . where we began our look at surviving life in a Small World:

◆ No family circumstance is unique.
◆ It's always too early to get off the boat.

What you're going through in your family is just another chapter in the cycle of dysfunction plaguing every family since Eden. I realize that doesn't help much—especially when your family's song is so dissonant, obnoxious, and repetitious that you're flat-out tired of all the drama.

Maybe God has been grooming you to help break your family free from the cycle of its own dysfunction. Like so many of the travelers we've visited in these pages, you can make a choice that leads your vessel in a new direction. It won't be easy, but it will be worth it.

If you're tired of that constantly repeating family refrain, don't jump ship. Instead, rewrite the part you intend to play in bringing your family's *stuckness* to an end.

Because that can happen.

And you *do* have a part to play . . . after all.

NOTES

CHAPTER 1

1. "Advanced Training at Zarephath," http://www.gracebiblefellowship-tx.org/Sermons/Elijah/3%20Advanced%20Training%20at%20Zarephath.rtf (accessed September 6, 2007).

2. Read about Paganini at www.paganini.com and http://en.wikipedia.org/wiki/Niccolo_paganini (accessed October 23, 2007).

CHAPTER 2

1. "Sex on the Brain," Mark Liberman, September 24, 2006, *The Boston Globe*, http://www.boston.com/news/globe/ideas/articles/2006/09/24/sex_on_the_brain?mode=PF (accessed August 23, 2007).

CHAPTER 4

1. "Mutt Gets $3 Million for Saving Drew Barrymore, and Who's the Richest Dog in the World?" December 20, 2002, http://dogsinthenews.com/issues/0212/articles/021220a.htm (accessed August 23, 2007).

2. Adam Clarke's commentary on www.studylight.org/com/acc/view.cgi?book=ge&chapter=041 (accessed September 30, 2007).

CHAPTER 6

1. Lance Armstrong, *It's Not About the Bike: My Journey Back to Life* (New York: G. P. Putnam's Sons, 2000), 3. Used by permission of G. P. Putnam's Sons, a division of Penguin Group (USA) Inc.

2. Rick Pitino, *Success Is a Choice: Ten Steps to Overachieving in Business and Life* (New York: Broadway Books, 1997), 230–231.

3. Ibid., 235.

4. Freda Crews, quoted by Carol Kent, *When I Lay My Isaac Down: Unshakable Faith in Unthinkable Circumstances* (Colorado Springs, CO: NavPress, 2004), 97.

5. Information in this section was taken from http://www.firstcoastnews.com/printfullstory.aspx?storyid=89208 and http://www.printthis.clickability.com/pt/cpt?action=cpt&title=BRI...FAID%3D%2F20070815%2FCOLO4%2F708150324%26imw%3DY&partnerID=162736 (accessed August 23, 2007).

CHAPTER 7

1. J. Hampton Keathley III, "The Principle of Nurture," http://www.bible.org/page.php?page_id=1379 (accessed September 5, 2007).

CHAPTER 8

1. http://www.ncbi.nlm.nih.gov/sites/entrez?cmd=Retrieve&db=PubMed&list_uids=10721277&dopt=AbstractPlus and http://www.prevent-abuse-now.com/stats.htm#Impact (accessed August 24, 2007).

2. http://mentalhealth.samhsa.gov/dadsarechamps/ (accessed August 23, 2007).

3. Gwen Morrison, "Time Together: Spending Quality Time With Your Teen," http://www.teenagerstoday.com/resources/articles/qualitytime.htm (accessed August 23, 2007).

CHAPTER 9

1. Referenced by Ron Deal, "Smart Stepparenting," http://www.family.org/parenting/A000000448.cfm (accessed August 24, 2007).

2. "Top Ten Sayings of Biblical Mothers," http://www.gentle.org/graceland/topten/topmom98.html (accessed August 23, 2007). But I confess, this list has a different number 1 than my original list, which I was unable to document but wanted to use. The number 1 for this list is really: "Jesus! Stop working on that old wood and come in and eat! You'd spend your life on that wood, if your father asked ya to!"

CHAPTER 10

1. Richard Lewis, *The Other Great Depression* (New York: Melonball Productions, Inc., 2000), 11–12.

2. Billy Graham. www.boycottliberalism.com/prayer.htm (accessed October 23, 2007).

3. Darren Rovell, "The Other Tiger That Lurks in the Woods," http://espn.go.com/sportsbusiness/s/2002/1031/1454033.html (accessed October 23, 2007).

CHAPTER 12

1. Information in this section was taken from Barry M. Horstman, "Runaway Cow a Folk Hero," http://www.cincypost.com/2002/feb/22/cow022202.html and staff report, "Moooovin' Along: The Official Chronicle of the Cow on the Run," http://old.wcpo.com/specials/2002/cow/ (accessed August 23, 2007).

ABOUT THE AUTHOR

To learn more about the author
please visit
www.koinacafe.com

RENOVATE YOUR LIFE

Let *Trading Places* help you make a change that will last forever. Courage alone won't sustain lasting change. True life change is a renovation only God can pull off, and He wants to pull it off — in partnership with you.

STEVE WYATT

TRADING PLACES

ALLOWING GOD TO RENOVATE YOUR LIFE

978-0-7847-1840-7

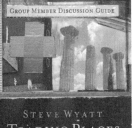

GROUP MEMBER DISCUSSION GUIDE

STEVE WYATT
TRADING PLACES
ALLOWING GOD TO RENOVATE YOUR LIFE

978-0-7847-1959-6

If you liked *Stuck in a Small World*,
we think you'll like these books!

For more information visit
www.standardpub.com
or call 1-800-543-1301.